A VOYAGE ROUND MY FATHER

John Mortimer

A VOYAGE ROUND MY FATHER

OBERON BOOKS
LONDON

First published by Methuen & Co. Ltd. in 1971

First published by Oberon Books Ltd.
in Collected Plays: Volume One in 2001
521 Caledonian Road, London N7 9RH
Tel: 020 7607 3637 / Fax: 020 7607 3629
e-mail: info@oberonbooks.com
www.oberonbooks.com

A catalogue record for this book is available from the British Library.

PB ISBN: 978-1-84002-657-3
E ISBN: 978-1-84943-808-7

Cover image by Dewynters plc, London

Visit www.oberonbooks.com to read more about all our books and to
buy them. You will also find features, author interviews and news of
any author events, and you can sign up for e-newsletters so that you're
always first to hear about our new releases.

*The text that follows was used for the production at
the Donmar Warehouse in June 2006
and was correct at the time of going to press.*

Characters

SON
(grown up)

FATHER

MOTHER

IRIS

SON
(as a boy)

RINGER

HEADMASTER

MATRON

JAPHET

HAM

REIGATE

REIGATE'S MOTHER

MISS COX

MISS BAKER

BOUSTEAD

JUDGE

THONG

DORIS

SPARKS

DIRECTOR

FIRST and SECOND ATS

ELIZABETH

GEORGE

MISS FERGUSON

MR MORROW

Another JUDGE

WITNESS

GIRL

FIRST and SECOND BOY

DOCTOR

Boys, Radio, Technicians, Robing-Room Man

This version of *A Voyage Round My Father* was first performed on 8 June 2006 at the Donmar Warehouse with the following company (in order of speaking):

FATHER	Derek Jacobi
SON	Dominic Rowan
IRIS/1ST ATS	Katie Warren
SON (boy)	Lewis Aaltonen / Charlie Bollands / Edward Jackson Keen
MOTHER	Joanna David
RINGER/THONG/DIRECTOR/MR MORROW	Neil Boorman
HEADMASTER	Christopher Benjamin
HAM/BOUSTEAD/GEORGE/DOCTOR	Osmund Bullock
JAPHET/SPARKS/1ST & 2ND JUDGE	Jamie de Courcey
REIGATE (boy)	Sonny Muharrem / Jolyon Price / Piers Stubbs
MISS BAKER/DORIS/WITNESS/REIGATE'S MOTHER	Sadie Shimmin
MISS COX/2ND ATS/MISS FERGUSON/MATRON	Lily Bevan
ELIZABETH	Natasha Little

Director	Thea Sharrock
Designer	Robert Jones
Lighting Designer	Peter Mumford
Sound Designer	Gregory Clarke

A Voyage Round My Father was first performed at Greenwich Theatre in 1970. A revised version was presented by Michael Codron Ltd. on 4 August 1971 at the Haymarket Theatre, London.

Act One

There is a trellis upstage-centre, wider at the top than the base, sweeping from the floor until it is out of sight in the flies; a bench, a ladder and a table with three chairs. Otherwise the stage is bare.

As the curtain rises, the SON (grown up) is sitting at the table reading his diary. The FATHER enters.

FATHER: Roses – not much of a show of roses.

SON: Not bad.

FATHER: Onions – hardly a bumper crop would you say?

SON: I suppose not.

>   *The FATHER, a man in his sixties, wearing a darned tweed suit, and carrying a clouded malacca walking-stick is, with blind eyes, inspecting his garden.*

FATHER: Earwigs at the dahlias. You remember; when you were a boy, you remember our great slaughter of earwigs?

SON: I remember.

FATHER: Do you see the dahlias?

SON: Yes.

FATHER: Describe them for me. Paint me the picture…

SON: Well, they're red – and yellow. And blowsy…

FATHER: (*Puzzled.*) Blowsy?

SON: They look sort of middle-aged – overripe.

FATHER: Earwig traps in place, are they?

SON: Yes. They're in place.

FATHER: When you were a boy, we often bagged a hundred earwigs in a single foray! Do you remember?

SON: I remember.

The SON moves away from the FATHER and speaks to the audience.

My father wasn't always blind. The three of us lived in a small house surrounded, as if for protection, by an enormous garden…

The MOTHER enters.

FATHER: Where's the boy got to?

MOTHER: Disappeared apparently.

FATHER: He's running wild.

SON: He was driven to the station, where he caught a train to London and the Law Courts, to his work as a barrister in a great hearse-like motor which he would no more have thought of replacing every year than he would have accepted a different kind of suit or a new gardening hat. As soon as possible he returned to the safety of the dahlias, and the ritual of the evening earwig-hunt. Visitors were rare and, if spotted, my father would move deeper into the foliage until the danger was past. Those were the days when my father could see – before I went away to school. When it was always a hot afternoon and a girl called Iris taught me to whistle.

The SON (as a boy) and a small girl called IRIS run on.

IRIS: Stick out your lips. Stick them out far. Go on. Farther. Much farther. Now blow. Not too hard. Blow gently. Gently. Don't laugh. Take it serious. Blow!

There is a sound of a whistle.

SON: (*As a boy.*) What was that?

IRIS: What do you mean – what was that?

SON: Someone whistled.

IRIS: It was you.

SON: Me?

IRIS: It was you whistling!

SON: I can do it! I know how to do it!

IRIS: Well, you've learnt something…

FATHER: The boy's running wild again.

MOTHER: Oh, I don't think so.

FATHER: Oh, yes, he is. And a good thing, too. When I was a boy in Africa, they sent me off – all by myself – to a small hotel up country to run wild for three months. I took my birthday cake with me and kept it under my bed. I well remember – (*He laughs.*) – when my birthday came round I took the cake out, sat on my bed, and ate it. That was my celebration!

MOTHER: He'll soon be going away to school…

FATHER: What did you say?

MOTHER: He'll be going away to school. We can't expect him to stay here – forever…

The FATHER gets a step-ladder and starts to walk up it, singing to himself.

FATHER: (*Singing.*) 'She was as bee-eautiful as a butterfly
        And as proud as a queen
        Was pretty little Polly Perkins of Paddington Green.
        I'm a broken-hearted milkman,
        In grief I'm arrayed,
        Through the keeping of the company
        Of a young servant maid.'

SON: (*Grown up.*) One day he bought a step-ladder for pruning the apple trees. He hit his head on the branch of a tree and the retinas left the balls of his eyes.

Suddenly, total black-out in which we hear the SON's voice.

That's the way I looked to my father from childhood upwards. That's how my wife and his grandchildren looked. My father was blind but we never mentioned it.

The lights fade up slowly to reveal the FATHER and MOTHER sitting round the breakfast table. The FATHER is clearly totally blind, the MOTHER is helping him cut up his toast.

He had a great disinclination to mention anything unpleasant. What was that? Courage, cowardice, indifference or caring too completely? Why didn't he blaspheme, beat his head against the pitch black sitting-room walls? Why didn't he curse God? He had a great capacity for rage – but never at the universe.

The SON (grown up) goes.

The family eat in silence until the FATHER suddenly bursts out.

FATHER: My egg! It's bloody runny! It's in a nauseating condition! What do you want to do? Choke me to death? (*Shouts.*) Have you all gone *mad*? Am I totally surrounded by *cretins*?

Another silence while they go on eating.

(*Singing.*) 'In six months she married,
    That hard-hearted girl,
    But it wasn't to a Viscount,
    It wasn't to an Earl,
    It wasn't to a Baronite,
    But a shade or two WUS!
    'Twas to the bow-legged conductor
    Of a twopenny bus!'

MOTHER: Marmalade?

FATHER: Thank you.

Silence.

The evolution of the horse was certainly a most tortuous process. None of your six-day nonsense! Six days' labour wouldn't evolve one primitive earthworm. Is the boy still here?

MOTHER: Please, dear. Don't be tactless.

FATHER: I thought he'd gone away to school.

MOTHER: *Pas devant le garçon.*

FATHER: What?

MOTHER: He doesn't like it mentioned.

FATHER: Well, either he's going away or he's not. I'm entitled to know. If he's here this evening he can help me out with the earwigs.

MOTHER: Mr Lean's going to drive him. *A trois heures et demi.*

FATHER: Half past three, eh?

MOTHER: Yes, dear. Mr Lean's going to drive him.

FATHER: (*To SON as a boy.*) You'll learn to construct an equilateral triangle and the Latin word for parsley. Totally useless information…

MOTHER: We really ought not to discourage the boy. (*To SON.*) You'll find the French very useful.

FATHER: What on earth for?

MOTHER: Going to France.

FATHER: What's he want to go to France for? There's plenty to do in the garden. The coffee's frozen! (*He drinks.*) It's like arctic mud!

MOTHER: Shall I make you some fresh?

FATHER: No. I like it. All education's perfectly useless. But it fills in the *time*. The boy can't sit around here all day until he gets old enough for marriage. He can't sit around – doing the crossword.

MOTHER: (*Laughing.*) Married! Plenty of time to think of that when he's learned to keep his bedroom tidy. The headmaster seemed rather charming.

FATHER: No one ever got a word of sense out of a school-master! If they *knew* anything they'd be out doing it. (*To the SON.*) That'll be your misfortune for the next few years. To be constantly rubbing up against second-rate minds.

MOTHER: At the start of each term apparently the new boys are given a little speech of welcome.

FATHER: Ignore that! Particularly if they offer you advice on the subject of life. At a pinch you may take their word on equilateral hexagons – but remember! Life's a closed book to schoolmasters.

MOTHER: We'll label your trunk this afternoon.

FATHER: You won't expect any advice from me, I hope? All advice's perfectly useless...

MOTHER: I've still got to mark your hockey stick.

FATHER: You're alone in the world, remember. No one can tell you what to do about it.

The SON (as a boy) starts to cry.

What's the matter with the boy?

MOTHER: (*Apparently incredulous.*) He's not crying!

FATHER: (*Coming out with some sound advice at last.*) Say the word 'rats'. No one can cry when they're saying the word 'rats'. It has to do with the muscles of the face.

SON: (*As a boy; trying to stop himself crying.*) Rats.

The FATHER, MOTHER and SON (as a boy) go.

SON: (*Grown up.*) Mr Ringer Lean was an ex-jockey who drove my father's antique Morris Oxford. He treated it as though it were a nervous stallion.

RINGER LEAN enters, carrying a school trunk on his shoulder.

RINGER: Car's gone lame. Going don't suit her. Shit-scared are you? Being sent away…

The SON (as a boy) comes on to the stage. He is wearing school uniform, carrying a suitcase and looking extremely depressed.

SON: (*Grown up.*) I was to be prepared for life. Complete with football boots, gym shoes, house shoes, shirts grey, shirts white, Bulldog Drummond, mint humbugs, boxing gloves, sponge bags, and my seating plans for all the London theatres…

The SON (as a boy) puts down the trunk and rests on it.

RINGER: They sent me away when I was your age. Newmarket Heath. Bound as a stable lad. Bloody terrified I was, at your age…

SON: Were you?

RINGER: Yes. They shouldn't send you away. You're going to develop too tall for a jockey.

SON: I don't think they want me to be a jockey…

RINGER: Broke a few bones, I did, when they sent me away. Ribs fractured. Collar-bone smashed. Pelvis pounded to pieces. Bad mounts. Bad Governors. Hey! When a Governor gets after you, you know what?

SON: What?

RINGER: Get up the hay-loft, and pull the ladder up after you. Because they can't climb. Oh, yes. Recall that. Governors can't climb. Often I've hid up the hay-loft one, two, three hours sometimes. 'Til the Governor got a winner, and change of heart. I've slept up there often. All right if the rats don't nip you.

SON: Thanks.

RINGER: Only bit of advice I got to give you – never avoid a mount. There was this lad at our stable – he avoided a half-broken two-year-old. Nasty tempered one with a duff eye. Well, this lad was shit-scared to ride it, you know what he did?

SON: No...

RINGER: Nobbled himself with a blunt razor-blade. Severed a tendon and then gangrene. Poor lad had to kiss his leg good-bye.

SON: It's not really a stable...

RINGER: So never try and nobble yourself. That's my advice. Or sterilize the blade. Hold it in a flame. Kills the germs on it!

SON: It's more a school than a stable...

RINGER: Oh well, wherever there's lads, I expect it's much the same...

SON: (*Grown up.*) My father had warned me – but this was far worse than I'd expected.

The lights change.

The STAFF and HEADMASTER enter.

HEADMASTER: Now, new boys. Stand up now. Let me look at you. Some day, some long distant day, you will be one-yearers, and then two-yearers, and then three-yearers. You will go away, and you will write letters, and I shall try hard to remember you. Then you'll be old boys. Old Cliffhangers. O.C.s you shall become, and the fruit of your loins shall attend the School by the Water. Leave the room the boy who laughed. The fruit of your loins shall return and stand here, even as you stand here. And we shall teach them. We shall give them sound advice. So that hungry generations of boys shall learn not to eat peas with their knives or butter their hair, or clean their finger-nails with bus tickets. You shall be taught to wash, to bowl straight and wipe your dirty noses. When you are in the sixth form you shall see something of golf. You will look on the staff as your friends. At all times you will call us by nicknames. I am Noah. My wife is Mrs Noah. You are the animals. My son Lance is Shem. Mr Pearce and Mr Box are Ham and Japhet. Matey is Matey. Mr Bingo Ollard is Mr Bingo Ollard. These mysteries have I expounded to you, oh litter of runts.

The lights change as the HEADMASTER, MATRON and JAPHET leave. Two BOYS move the bench into position. The SON (as a boy) brings on a blackboard. HAM starts drawing a right-angle triangle on it.

SON: (*Grown up, to the audience.*) The masters who taught us still suffered from shell-shock and battle fatigue. Some had shrapnel lodged in their bodies and the classroom would turn, only too easily, into another Paschendale.

The SON (as a boy) and another boy of his own age, named REIGATE, sit on the bench in front of HAM's blackboard, watching him complete his drawing of Pythagoras' theorem.

HAM: The square on the longest side of a right-angled bloody triangle is – is what, boy?

SON: (*Standing up.*) I don't know…

HAM: (*Suddenly yelling.*) Straff you, boy. Bomb and howitzer and straff the living daylights out of you. God bomb you to hell! (*He throws books at the SON.*) Get your tin hat on. It's coming over now! It's equal to the square… What square, you unfortunate cretin? On the other two sides. Right-angled bloody triangle! Straff you, boy! Bomb and howitzer you! God bomb you to hell! All right. All right. War's over… Armistice day. Demob. I suppose you want compensation?

The BOYS pick up the books.

SON: If you like, sir.

HAM: How many books did I throw?

SON: Six, sir. Not counting the duster.

HAM: Threepence a book and say a penny the duster. Is that fair?

SON: I'd say so, sir.

HAM: Is that one-and-six?

SON: I think it's one and sevenpence, sir.

SON: (*Grown up.*) From Ham I learnt the healing power of money…

FATHER enters as HAM and the BOYS go, HAM taking the blackboard.

FATHER: I am writing to you from outside the President's Court at the start of a divorce case. Like all divorce cases, this one is concerned with sex, which you will find to be a subject filled with comic relief. Pearson Dupray, K.C., who is agin me in this case is not a foeman worthy of my steel. He will no doubt fumble his cross-examination and may even fail to prove my adultery – although God knows – I have had inclination and opportunity to spare.

JAPHET, strumming a ukelele, appears upstage.

JAPHET: 'Hallelujah I'm a bum
　　　　Hallelujah Bum again
　　　　Hallelujah give us a hand out…
　　　　To revive us again…'

FATHER: Like you, I shall today be rubbing up against a second-rate mind…

SON: (*Grown up.*) Japhet, the second master, did his unsuccessful best to impart polish.

JAPHET: (*Sings.*) 'Hallelujah – I'm a bum…'

　Do you know what a bum is?

SON: (*As a boy.*) Yes, sir.

JAPHET: Good.

> 'Hallelujah. Bum again –
> Hallelujah, give us a hand out…'

Now look. Nobody is going to laugh if you just use two simple chords. You see. Like this – and this. That's all. Just two simple chords. Always. For every tune. You take my tip, and look as if you know what you're doing. Nobody's going to laugh. Oh, by the way, you don't tie that tie of yours properly. Remind me to teach you to tie your tie, will you? Yes, you take my advice and sing in the back of your nose – so it sounds as if you've crossed the States by railroad. (*He starts to sing through his nose to the ukelele.*)

> 'Oh, why don't you work
> Like other men do?
> How the heck can I work
> If there's no work to do…?
> Hallelujah. I'm a bum!'

You see. Just two simple chords, and don't get ambitious.

SON: No, I won't, sir.

JAPHET: And do remember about that tie. It's really very easy, you know. Right over left, over left, over right, over all, up the back and down the front, and that way you get a big knot. The way *He* wears it.

SON: He?

JAPHET: The King, of course.

SON: Oh, yes, sir – of course.

JAPHET: The King and I – we've got a lot in common.

SON: Yes, sir.

JAPHET: Same tie – same trouble.

SON: What trouble's that, sir?

JAPHET: Woman trouble. Deep, deep trouble. Just like the jolly old King…

JAPHET exits with his ukelele. The SON takes a letter out of his pocket and reads it.

SON: (*Grown up.*) I knew what he was talking about. He was talking about Lydia, a pale little red-headed girl who smelt vaguely of mothballs and who made our beds. The King and Japhet were both tussling with the problems from which my father made his living.

FATHER: You will probably be pleased to hear that I won Jimpson v. Jimpson, the wife being found guilty of infidelity in the front of the Daimler parked in Hampstead Garden Suburb. A vital part of the evidence consisted of footprints on the dashboard…

REIGATE comes in, bored, his hands in his pockets, and wanders near the SON. The SON, reading the letter, does not notice him.

The co-respondent was condemned in costs. My final speech lasted two hours and I made several jokes. At home we have been pricking out Korean chrysanthemums and making marmalade. Unusually large plague of earwigs this summer. Ever your loving father…

REIGATE: (*To the SON.*) Do you get many letters from home?

The FATHER and MOTHER get up and the MOTHER leads the FATHER out.

The SON puts the letter hurriedly back in the envelope.

SON: Hello, Reigate. Once a week, I expect.

REIGATE: Keep the envelopes.

SON: For the stamps?

REIGATE: To put the fish in, on Saturday nights. The fish is disgusting. Put it in the envelope and post it down the bogs.

SON: Why in envelopes?

REIGATE: Well, you just can't put bits of fish, not straight in your pocket. (*He pauses.*) Is your mother slim?

SON: Fairly slim.

Pause.

REIGATE: Is your father good at golf?

SON: Pretty good.

REIGATE: My mother's slim as a bluebell.

SON: Well, mine's quite slim too, really. She goes to cocktail parties.

REIGATE: As slim as a bluebell! With yellow eyes.

SON: Yellow?

REIGATE: Like a panther.

SON: Oh, I see.

REIGATE: Very small feet. High heels, of course. Does your mother wear high heels?

SON: Whenever she goes to cocktail parties. She wears them then.

REIGATE: My mother wears high heels. *Even at breakfast.* Of course she's slim as a bluebell…

SON: (*Grown up.*) But November the eleventh brought embarrassing revelations. We were able to see those from whose loins, as Noah would say, we had actually sprung.

The SON (as a boy) and REIGATE part and move to opposite sides of the stage. On his side, the SON is met by the MOTHER and the FATHER, come down for the Armistice Day service. REIGATE is met by his MOTHER, a short, dumpy woman in a hat. HAM, JAPHET and the MATRON enter. The MATRON has a tray of poppies, the other grown-ups have umbrellas. Finally the HEADMASTER enters.

HEADMASTER: Let us pray…

The PARENTS and BOYS form a congregation. MRS REIGATE closes her eyes in an attitude of devotion. The FATHER blows his nose loudly. REIGATE stares across at him. The SON (as a boy) looks at his FATHER in an agony of embarrassment, and then continues a close and somewhat surprised study of REIGATE's MOTHER.

Oh Lord, inasmuch as we are paraded now on Lower School Field on this, the Armistice Day, November the eleventh, nineteteen hundred and thirty-six, help us to remember those O.C.s who fell upon alien soil in the late Great Match. Grant us their spirit, we beseech Thee, that we may go 'over the top' to our Common Entrance and our Football Fixtures, armed with the 'cold steel' of Thy Holy Word. Give us, if Thy will be done, the Great Opportunity to shed our Blood for our Country and our Beloved School, and fill us with that feeling of Sportsmanship which led our fathers to fix bayonets and play until the last whistle blew. We will now sing the concluding hymn on your hymn sheets: 'God of our Fathers, known of old.'

REIGATE's MOTHER is singing in a rich patriotic contralto. The FATHER is singing, and his mouth seems to be moving in a different time from the rest of the congregation. Gradually what he is singing becomes painfully clear over and above the reverberation of the hymn.

FATHER: (*Singing.*) '…bee-eautiful as a butterfly
        And as proud as a queen
        Was pretty little Polly Perkins
        Of Paddington Green.'

Both the FATHER's song and the hymn come to an end at the same time.

ALL: Amen.

The HEADMASTER is saying goodbye, shaking parents' hands.

HEADMASTER: How do you do, Mrs Reigate? How very nice to see you again.

The HEADMASTER and the parents go.

SON: (*Grown up.*) Our parents, it was obvious, needed a quick coating of romance.

SON: (*As a boy.*) She didn't look much like a panther.

REIGATE: Who?

SON: And your mother wasn't exactly like a bluebell, either.

REIGATE: My mother? You've never seen my mother.

SON: Of course I have.

REIGATE: Oh, don't be so simple. That good, honest woman isn't my real mother.

SON: (*Puzzled.*) Noah called her 'Mrs Reigate'. I heard him distinctly.

REIGATE: Noah only knows what's good for him to know. That was no more my mother than you are.

SON: Who was she then?

REIGATE: Just a dear, good, old soul who promised to look after me.

SON: When?

REIGATE: When they smuggled me out of Russia, after the revolution. They smuggled me out in a wickerwork trunk. I was ten days and nights on the rack in the carriage of the Siberian Railway. Then we got to Paris…

SON: I thought Siberia…

REIGATE: They tried to shoot us in Paris. Me and my brother. But we got away, across the frozen river.

SON: I understood Siberia was in the other direction.

REIGATE: And escaped to England. This honest chemist and wife took care of us. Swear you won't tell anyone?

SON: All right.

REIGATE: By the blood of my father?

SON: If you like. I just heard from my parents, actually. Something pretty sensational.

REIGATE: Oh, yes?

SON: I think they're probably – getting divorced.

REIGATE: (*Interested.*) Honestly?

SON: Honestly.

REIGATE: Why? Are they unfaithful?

SON: Oh, always. And I told you. My mother goes to cocktail parties…

REIGATE: (*Admiringly.*) You'll be having a broken home, then?

SON: (*Casually.*) Oh, yes. I expect I will…

The two BOYS go together.

SON: (*Grown up, to the audience.*) But when I got home, nothing had changed. My home remained imperturbably intact. And, in the bracken on the common, Iris had built me a house.

The lights come up on another part of the stage where IRIS is kneeling, building a house under the upturned garden table.

IRIS: What do you learn at school?

SON: We learn Latin.

IRIS: What else?

SON: Greek.

IRIS: Say, 'Good morning, what a very nice morning,' in Latin.

SON: I don't know how.

IRIS: All right. In Greek…

SON: I can't.

IRIS: Why not?

SON: They're not those sort of languages.

IRIS: What's the point of them, then?

SON: They train – the mind…

IRIS: How's your Mum and Dad?

SON: Quarrelling.

IRIS: I never see them quarrel.

SON: Oh, it's life… They come back from parties, and they quarrel. Don't ask me to explain.

IRIS: I didn't.

SON: Well – don't.

IRIS: I shan't.

SON: It's just possible, they're not my parents. A very honest couple, but not…

IRIS: Of course they're your parents. Don't be ignorant.

SON: I'm not ignorant.

IRIS: What do you know, then?

SON: I know the second person plural future passive of *rogo*.

IRIS: What is it?

SON: *Rogobamini.*

IRIS: What's that mean?

SON: It doesn't mean anything. It's just the future passive of *rogo* – that's all it is…

IRIS: (*After a pause; pointing to the house.*) Why don't we get in now?

SON: (*Shrugs his shoulders.*) What for?

IRIS: To play Mothers and Fathers.

SON: I think I might find that a bit painful, well, what with the situation at home. Anyway, I haven't got time.

IRIS: Haven't you?

SON: Someone's coming over to see me today.

IRIS: Who's that?

SON: His name's Reigate, actually.

IRIS: Don't you want to be Mothers and Fathers... Tell you what, I'll let you see...

(*She lifts up her skirt.*)

SON: No, thank you. Reigate's coming to stay...

IRIS goes. REIGATE comes in.

REIGATE: You start then.

SON: Bill...

REIGATE: Who is it...?

SON: It's me, Bill. It's Harry.

MOTHER enters.

REIGATE: Harry!

MOTHER: Where do you want us to sit?

SON: In the stalls.

REIGATE: What comes next?

SON: I can't see you, old fellow.

REIGATE: I can't see you, old fellow. Then what?

SON: You were supposed to learn your lines!

FATHER enters.

MOTHER: There now, darling. Did you have a good rest?

FATHER: What's good about a rest? 'My best of rest is sleep, and that thou oft provok'st, yet grossly fearest thy death which is no more.'

MOTHER: There's going to be a little surprise.

REIGATE: (*To the SON; suspiciously.*) Can't see much sign of divorce in this family.

SON: They're putting on a show – for the visitor.

FATHER: (*Pleased.*) Is something happening?

MOTHER: It's the boy talking to Reigate.

FATHER: To whom?

MOTHER: To Reigate – his friend.

FATHER: (*Incredulously.*) The boy has a friend? Welcome, Reigate! What's Reigate like, eh? Paint me the picture.

MOTHER: Well, he's quite small, and...

SON: And he's really Russian...

FATHER: (*Impressed.*) Russian, eh? Well, that's something of an achievement. (*He pauses.*) When I was at school I never minded the lessons. I just resented having to work so terribly hard at playing. They don't roast you at school nowadays, I suppose? I can't think what I'm paying all that money for if they don't roast you from time to time...

MOTHER: Do you like school, Reigate?

REIGATE: It's all right. The Headmaster makes us call him Noah.

SON: And his son is Shem.

REIGATE: And we have to call Mr Box and Mr Pearce Ham and Japhet. And we're the animals.

SON: And Mr Bingo Ollard is Mr Bingo Ollard.

FATHER: (*Gloomily.*) Didn't I warn you? Second-rate minds.

REIGATE: Now we're going to do something to keep you from thinking of your great unhappiness.

MOTHER: Our unhappiness…

FATHER: What did he say?

MOTHER: They're going to put on an entertainment.

FATHER: Oh, I like entertainment. When's it to be?

SON: This afternoon.

MOTHER: Well, you'd better hurry up, because Mr Lean's coming to drive you back to school at six. (*She giggles gently.*) Whatever will they think of…

The SON and REIGATE exit.

FATHER: What're you laughing at?

MOTHER: At Reigate?

FATHER: Who on earth's Reigate?

MOTHER: I told you, dear. The boy's friend.

FATHER: Is this Reigate, then, something of a wit?

The SON and REIGATE enter with a hamper.

MOTHER: He does come out with some killing suggestions.

REIGATE: (*Dignified.*) We're going to do a play.

FATHER: What is it? Something out of the *Boy's Own*?

SON: I wrote it.

FATHER: You what?

MOTHER: I'm sure Reigate helped. Didn't you Reigate?

SON: He didn't help.

MOTHER: What are you actually supposed to be? Two little clowns?

REIGATE: Actually, we're two subalterns. Killed on the Somme, actually.

They take coats, caps and a belt from the hamper and put them on.

FATHER: They'll soon be giving us war again. When it comes, avoid the temptation to do anything heroic. What's going on? Make it vivid.

The BOYS exit and return with barbed wire which they set up.

MOTHER: They're bringing in some of your barbed wire.

FATHER: My what?

MOTHER: Your barbed wire.

FATHER: Oh, put it back again, won't you. We don't want the cows everywhere.

MOTHER: Reigate's got your greatcoat, and the boy's wearing your old Sam Browne.

FATHER: How killing!

SON: Lights out! Curtain up!

MOTHER: Well, we can see Reigate's artistic! He's giving a very lively performance.

REIGATE: Actually we're ghosts.

FATHER: Ghosts, eh? What's happening now?

SON: We're meeting after the bombardment.

MOTHER: It's after the bombardment.

FATHER: How very killing!

SON: Bill…

REIGATE: Who is it…?

SON: It's me, Bill. It's Harry.

REIGATE: Harry! I can't see you, old fellow. It's this damn gas, everywhere. Take my hand.

SON: Where are you?

REIGATE: Out here – by the wire. Listen.

SON: What?

REIGATE: They've stopped straffing. I say, if ever we get back to the old country –

SON: What?

REIGATE: – I want you to marry Helen.

SON: You said you'd never let Helen marry a chap who'd funked the top board at Roehampton…

REIGATE: N'you mind what I said, Harry. I saw you today on the north redoubt; you were in there, batting for England! You shall have my little sister, boy. My hand on it.

SON: I can't feel your hand, Bill.

REIGATE: I can't see you, Harry.

SON: I'm cold…

REIGATE: I'm afraid we'll never see England again.

SON: What's the matter with us, Bill?

REIGATE: (*Beginning to laugh.*) We're dead, old fellow. Can't you understand? We're both of us – dead!

FATHER: Dead! How killing!

The play over, the BOYS bow to the MOTHER and FATHER.

MOTHER: That was splendid! Now we must clear away all this barbed wire, but mind your hands.

The BOYS exit with the hamper and costumes, and the barbed wire.

FATHER: (*Serious.*) Dead. You know I didn't want to be dead. I never wanted that. When your mother and I got married – at Saffron Walden, they were just about to pack me off to France. Bands. Troopships. Flowers thrown at you... and dead in a fortnight. I didn't want to have anything to do with it. And then, the day before I was due to sail my old Major drew me aside and said, 'You're just married, old fellow. No particular sense in being dead!' He'd found me a post in the Inland Waterways! That's advice to you, if they look like giving us war. Get yourself a job in the Inland Waterways...

FATHER exits. REIGATE and the SON (as a boy) enter.

REIGATE: Your parents seem to be getting on quite well.

SON: They pretend – for me.

REIGATE: And your mother didn't seem to drink very much either.

SON: Not 'til the evenings.

REIGATE: You know? I'll tell you something about your father...

SON: What?

REIGATE: He can't see. He's blind, isn't he?

SON: (*Grown up.*) It was a question our family never asked. Naturally I didn't answer it.

Dance music starts.

JAPHET enters with a gramophone on a trolley.

JAPHET: And – slow, slow, quick, quick, slow – and chassis – chassis! How do you expect to get through life if you

31

can't even do the foxtrot? That's the trouble with education today. It never teaches you anything worth knowing. Do you know, there are boys here who can't even tie their ties, let alone tango… Come on. Sorry you're leaving?

SON: Not altogether…

JAPHET: I'm leaving too. Perhaps you heard…?

SON: Yes, sir, I know. Lydia left yesterday. We had to make our own beds this morning.

The music stops.

JAPHET: Yes. Lydia's left. I've resigned. So has the poor old King.

SON: Him as well…?

JAPHET: He broadcast this afternoon. We all heard him on Noah's radiogram. The King has given up everything for love. I told you we had a lot in common. Take my advice. Don't give up everything for love…

SON: No, I won't, sir.

JAPHET: It's just not on – that's all. Just simply not on…

SON: You coming to Noah's talk, sir? It's for all of us leavers.

JAPHET: The one where he tells you the facts of life…?

SON: Yes, sir. I think that's the one.

JAPHET: No. I shall stay away. I've heard quite enough about *them* to be going on with…

The HEADMASTER appears, wearing a tweed jacket with leather patches and smoking a pipe. REIGATE comes in and sits on the floor gazing up at him respectfully. JAPHET packs up his gramophone and goes. The SON moves away.

HEADMASTER: You are the leavers! In a month or two you will go on to Great Public Schools, away from this cosy little establishment.

The SON arrives and stands and knocks.

Come in, you're disturbing everybody. Shut the door, boy.
Most terrible draught. Ah now, before I forget, Mrs Noah
and I will be pleased to see you all to tea on Sunday. A
trifling matter of anchovy paste sandwiches! Do you hear
that, eh, Reigate? All boys to come with clean finger-nails,
no boy to put butter on his hair.

REIGATE: Please, sir?

HEADMASTER: Yes, Reigate.

REIGATE: Why aren't we to put butter on our hair?

HEADMASTER: Ah! Good question. I'm glad you asked me
that! We had that trouble with the native regiments. They
used to lick their hair down with butter. It went rancid in
the hot weather. Unpleasant odour on parade. There's no
law against a drop of water on the comb. Now, what was
I going to tell you? Ah! I was warning you about dreams.
You'll have them. Oh, certainly you'll have them. And in
the morning you may say to yourselves, 'You rotter! To
have a dream like that!' Well, you can't help it. That's all.
You simply can't help them. Not dreams. Of course, if you
are awake you can do something about it. You can change
into a pair of shorts and go for a run across country. Or
you can get into the bath, and turn on the cold tap. You
can always do that. Your housemaster will understand.
He'll understand if you should've been up to a French
lesson, or Matins or some such thing. Simply say, 'Sir, I
had to have a bath,' or go for a run, or whatever it is. Just
say to Mr Raffles, or Humphrey Stiggler, or Percy Parr, just
say to Mr Raffles or Mr Parr, dependent on which school
you're at of course, 'that, sir, is what I felt the need to do.'
He'll understand perfectly. Now, another thing! When
sleeping, always lie on the right side. Not on the face, for
obvious reasons. Not on the left side. Stops the heart. Not
on the back, brings on dreams. Just the right side – all
the time. Now, to the most serious problem you're likely
to run up against. Friends. You may find that a boy from

another class, or a house even, comes up to you and says, 'Let's be friends,' or even offers you a slice of cake. That's a simple one, a perfectly simple one to deal with. You just say very loudly, 'I'm going to tell the housemaster.' Straight away. No hesitation about it. Remember, the only drawback to our Great Public School system is unsolicited cake – have you got this very clear? Go straight and tell the housemaster.

SON: (*Grown up.*) It wasn't until later that I realized that the Headmaster had been trying to advise us on a subject which my father used to often bring up unexpectedly, in the middle of tea.

FATHER: Sex! It's been greatly overrated by the poets. I never had many mistresses with thighs like white marble.

MOTHER: Would you like your biscuit now, dear?

SON: (*Grown up.*) Now what did he mean? Did he mean that he'd had many mistresses without especially marmoreal thighs – or few mistresses of any sort?

FATHER: 'Change in a trice
　　　　The lilies and languors of virtue
　　　　For the raptures and roses of vice!'

Where's my bloody biscuit?

MOTHER: I put it in your saucer.

FATHER: 'From their lips have thy lips taken fever?'
　　　　'Is the breath of them hot in thy hair…?'

SON: (*Grown up, to the audience.*) What did he know of the sharp uncertainties of love?

FATHER: (*Suddenly laughing.*) 'Is the breath of them hot in thy hair?' How perfectly revolting it sounds! Sex is pretty uphill work, if you want my opinion.

SON: I don't agree.

FATHER: You don't agree?

SON: I don't happen to agree.

FATHER: Who's that?

MOTHER: The boy!

SON: I don't think sex has been overrated exactly.

FATHER: I'll tell you a story. A lover, a wife and an angry husband...

MOTHER: (*Calmly.*) Not that one, dear. (*To the SON.*) You'll have some tea?

FATHER: Why ever not?

MOTHER: It's not very suitable. (*To the SON; vaguely.*) Do you like sugar? I always forget.

SON: Nothing.

FATHER: The husband returns and discovers all! He summons the lover into the dining-room. The wife waits, trembling, terrified, for the sounds of fighting, the smashing of crockery. Silence. She tiptoes down the stairs. There's the husband and the lover side by side at the dining-table, perfectly contented, drinking light ale. Suddenly, she bursts out at both of them – 'You ungrateful brutes!' They both listen as the door slams behind her. Then they open another bottle of light ale.

Pause. The SON looks down.

SON: Did that really happen? I don't believe that ever really happened. We've got some new neighbours.

FATHER: It's the ridiculous inconvenience of sex. That's what they never write about. New neighbours? Perhaps we'd better plant some more poplars.

SON: Miss Baker and Miss Cox.

FATHER: Who?

MOTHER: Two ladies who run the new bookshop. By the station. Apparently he went in to buy a book and they found him *simpatico*...

FATHER: He hasn't invited them back here, has he?

The SON does not answer.

He hasn't encouraged them to 'drop in', for a glass of sherry?

No answer.

If he has I shall lie doggo! I shall go to earth in the West Copse, I promise you.

MOTHER: He didn't say he was bringing them here.

FATHER: Well, if he does, I shall disappear without a trace. Doesn't he know we dread visitors? Poor boy! He'll miss the evening foray after earwigs. What exactly did he say?

MOTHER: He didn't say anything.

FATHER: Well, I think I'd better go and cut off deadheads – at the far end of the border.

FATHER and MOTHER exit.

SON: Miss Baker and Miss Cox! One was as soft and feathery as Carol Lombard. In the other I found Joan Crawford's merciless sensuality. They both smelt of Imperial Leather soap and talked of distant days in the South of France. I spent afternoons deciding which I should first seduce.

MISS COX and MISS BAKER enter.

MISS COX: I could have kissed you when you first came into our shop.

SON: Could you really?

MISS BAKER: And actually bought a book!

The SON wheels on a trolley with drinks and a radio.

MISS COX: Most people come in for pamphlets. A hundred things to do with dried egg – published by the Ministry of Food. Is your family out?

SON: I'm afraid so. Would you like a drink?

MISS BAKER: Please.

MISS COX: I'd adore a Pernod. Bill and I got used to Pernod in Cassis.

SON: Who's Bill?

MISS BAKER: I'm Bill. She's Daphne. (*She looks out across the garden.*)

SON: I'm afraid we're out of Pernod!

MISS COX: Sherry would be lovely. Did you say your family were out?

SON: I'm afraid so. Cocktail parties.

MISS COX: We've never actually met your father.

MISS BAKER: No. We looked over the gate one evening and shouted. He was busy doing something with a bucket.

SON: Probably the earwigs.

MISS COX: What?

SON: He drowns earwigs every night. Cheerio! It's quite a small house really, isn't it? I mean, you know, when you consider the size of the garden. (*Pause.*) Oh! (*Pause.*)

SON switches on the radio. Charles Trenet starts to sing.

I adore Charles Trenet, don't you?

MISS COX: Bill and I once danced with Charles Trenet. In Cassis.

RADIO: (*Making a sudden announcement.*) What do I do if I come across a German or Italian broadcast when tuning my wireless? I say to myself: 'Now this blighter wants me to listen to him, so I'm going to turn this blighter off!'

The SON turns off the radio.

MISS BAKER: Bloody war. I've been called up!

MISS COX: Bill's been called up. They're putting her on the land.

MISS BAKER: I'll probably ruin the crops.

MISS COX: It's the war, Bill. We all have to make sacrifices. (*To the SON.*) Bill doesn't care much for this war. We were more keen on the war in Spain.

MISS BAKER: They've got me down for a pig farm, near Godalming.

MISS COX: All our friends were awfully keen on the war in Spain. Stephen Spender and all that jolly lot.

SON: Oh. I love Stephen Spender.

MISS COX: I expect you'll go into the Fire Service.

SON: Why?

MISS COX: All our friends go into the Fire Service.

MISS BAKER: They get a lot of time for writing, waiting about between fires.

MOTHER passes through with a bucket of water.

MOTHER: We forgot the bucket for the drowning.

FATHER: (*Off.*) Have you abandoned me?

MOTHER: Coming, darling.

The MOTHER exits.

MISS BAKER: Well, I expect you'd like us to…

SON: Please, my father always says that in time of war one should avoid the temptation to do anything heroic.

MISS COX: One day we'd like to meet him.

FATHER: (*Off.*) Did you manage to get rid of them?

MOTHER: (*Off.*) Ssh!

MISS COX: The Fire Service. That's where you'll end up. It gives everyone far more time to write.

MISS BAKER: Is that what you're going to be then, a writer?

MISS COX, MISS BAKER and SON exit.

FATHER and MOTHER enter.

MOTHER: Isn't there an easier way of getting rid of earwigs?

FATHER: Sometimes I think women don't understand anything. Easier way!

SON enters. MOTHER exits with the trolley and returns.

MOTHER: Did you enjoy your visitors, dear?

FATHER: (*After a pause.*) Is that you?

SON: Yes, it's me.

FATHER: What're you doing?

SON: Helping you.

FATHER: Consider the persistence of the earwig. Each afternoon it feasts on our dahlia blooms. Each evening it climbs into our flower-pots to sleep. We empty the flower-pots and drown the earwigs – yet still they come. Nature's remorseless.

SON: I may be a writer…

FATHER: If we did this for one million years all over the world, do you think we would make some small dent in the pattern of evolution? Would we produce an earwig that could swim? (*After a pause.*) You'd be far better off in the Law…

SON: I'd like to write…

FATHER: You'll have plenty of spare time! My first five years in chambers, I did nothing but *The Times* crossword puzzle. Besides, if you were only a writer, who would you rub shoulders with? (*With contempt.*) Other writers? You'll be far better off in the Law.

SON: I don't know…

FATHER: No brilliance is needed in the Law. Nothing but common sense, and relatively clean finger-nails. Another thing, if you were a writer and married, think of your poor unfortunate wife…

SON: What?

FATHER: Well, she'd have you at home all day! In carpet slippers. Drinking tea and stumped for words! You'd be far better off down the tube each morning, and off to the Law Courts. Now, how many have we bagged today?

SON: (*Looking down into the bucket.*) About a hundred.

FATHER: A moderate bag, I'd say. Merely moderate. You know, the law of husband and wife may seem idiotic at first sight. Bet when you get to know it, it can exercise a vague, medieval charm. Learn a little Law, won't you? Just to please me.

FATHER exits.

SON: It was my father's way to offer the Law to me – the great, stone column of authority which has been dragged by an adulterous, careless, negligent and half-criminal humanity down the ages – as if it were a small mechanical toy which might occupy half an hour on a rainy afternoon. (*To the audience.*) He never used a white stick – but his clouded malacca was heard daily, tapping the stone corridors of the Law Courts. He had no use for therapy, dogs nor training, nor did he adapt himself to his condition. He simply pretended that nothing had happened.

SON goes. MR BOUSTEAD enters, robed and carrying his wig. The JUDGE enters and sits.

BOUSTEAD: Good morning.

MOTHER: Good morning.

FATHER: Who's that?

MOTHER: It's Mr Boustead, dear. He's for the husband.

FATHER: Agin me, Bulstrode. Are you agin me?

BOUSTEAD: Boustead.

FATHER: Excuse me. Boustead, of course. Where are you?

BOUSTEAD: Here, I'm here…

FATHER: I have studied your case pretty closely and I have a suggestion to make which you might find helpful.

BOUSTEAD: Really?

FATHER: What I am suggesting, entirely for your assistance, of course – is that you might like – my dear boy – to throw in your hand. Now, is that a help to you?

BOUSTEAD: Certainly not! I'd say we have some pretty valuable evidence…

The lights change.

In the witness-box appears MR THONG, a private detective of crafty appearance.

BOUSTEAD stands questioning him. The MOTHER leads the FATHER to his seat and sits behind him.

Now from the vantage point which you have already described, Mr Thong, will you tell my Lord and the Jury exactly what you saw?

The FATHER turns and speaks in a loud stage-whisper to the MOTHER.

FATHER: Throat spray!

The MOTHER puts a small throat spray into the FATHER's hand. THONG consults his notebook.

BOUSTEAD: Yes, Mr Thong, in your own words.

FATHER: (*In a loud whisper.*) Thank you.

THONG: (*Monotonously, reading his notebook.*) From my point of vantage, I was quite clearly able to see inside the kitchen window…

BOUSTEAD: Yes?

THONG: And…

The FATHER opens his mouth and starts, very loudly, to spray his throat.

JUDGE: Speak up, Mr Thong, I can't hear.

THONG: My Lord. I was able to distinguish clearly the respondent.

JUDGE: Yes…

THONG: In the act of…

The FATHER works the throat spray very loudly.

BOUSTEAD: If my learned friend would allow us to hear the evidence…

FATHER: (*Puts down the throat spray and whispers deafeningly to BOUSTEAD.*) I'm so sorry. My dear boy, if this is the valuable evidence you told me about, I shall be as quiet – as the tomb…!

BOUSTEAD: (*Firmly.*) Mr Thong.

FATHER: (*Half rising to address the JUDGE.*) By all means, my Lord. Let us hear this *valuable* evidence.

JUDGE: Very well.

THONG: I distinctly saw them…

The FATHER drops his malacca cane with a clatter.

FATHER: Oh, my God. How can I apologize.

JUDGE: Distinctly saw them what?

THONG: Kissing and cuddling, my Lord.

BOUSTEAD: And then…

THONG: The light was extinguished…

BOUSTEAD: Where?

THONG: In the kitchen.

BOUSTEAD: And a further light appeared?

THONG: In the bedroom.

JUDGE: For a moment?

THONG: Merely momentarily, my Lord.

BOUSTEAD: So…

THONG: So the house was shrouded in darkness. And the co-respondent, and this is the point that struck us, had not emerged.

BOUSTEAD: And you kept up observation until…

THONG: Approximately, dawn.

BOUSTEAD: (*Very satisfied, as he sits down.*) Thank you, Mr Thong.

The FATHER rises, clattering. Folds his hands on his stomach, gazes sightlessly at MR THONG and then allows a long pause during which MR THONG stirs uncomfortably. Then he starts quietly, slowly working himself up into a climax.

FATHER: Mr Thong, what price did you put on the valuable evidence?

THONG: I don't know what you mean…

FATHER: You have been paid, haven't you, to give it?

THONG: I'm a private enquiry agent…

FATHER: A professional witness?

THONG: Charging the usual fee.

FATHER: Thirty pieces of silver?

BOUSTEAD: (*Rising; indignantly.*) My Lord, I object. This is outrageous.

JUDGE: Perhaps that was not entirely relevant.

BOUSTEAD subsides.

FATHER: Then let me ask you something which is very relevant. Which goes straight to the secret heart of this wretched conspiracy. Where was this lady's husband during your observations?

THONG: Captain Waring?

FATHER: Yes, Captain Waring.

THONG: He had accompanied me…

FATHER: Why?

THONG: For purpose of…

FATHER: For purpose of what…?

THONG: Identification…

FATHER: And how long did he remain with you?

THONG: As long as observation continued…

FATHER: 'Til dawn…?

THONG: Until approximately five-thirty a.m.

FATHER: And did he not storm the house? Did he not beat upon the door? Did he not seize his wife's paramour by the throat and hurl him into the gutter?

THONG: According to my notebook. No.

FATHER: And according to your notebook, was he enjoying himself?

BOUSTEAD: (*Driven beyond endurance, rising to protest.*) Really…!

FATHER: Please, Mr Bulstrode! I've sat here for three days! Like patience on a monument! Whilst a series of spiteful, mean, petty, trumped-up, sickening and small-minded charges are tediously paraded against the unfortunate woman I represent. And now, when I rise to cross-examine – *I will not be interrupted.*

JUDGE: Gentlemen! Gentlemen, please. (*To the FATHER.*) What was your question?

FATHER: I've forgotten it. My learned friend's interruption has had the effect he no doubt intended and I have forgotten my question!

BOUSTEAD: This is intolerable…

FATHER: Ah. Now I've remembered it again. Did he enjoy the night, Thong, in this field – from which he was magically able to overlook his own kitchen…?

THONG: This plot of waste ground…

FATHER: Up a tree, was he?

THONG: What?

FATHER: Was he perched up a tree?

THONG: We had stepped up, into the lower branches.

FATHER: Was it the naked eye?

THONG: Pardon?

FATHER: Was he viewing this distressing scene by aid of the naked eye?

THONG: Captain Waring had brought a pair of field-glasses.

FATHER: His racing-glasses?

THONG: I…

JUDGE: Speak up, Mr Thong.

THONG: I imagine he used them for racing, my Lord.

FATHER: You see, Captain Waring has already given evidence in this court.

BOUSTEAD: (*Ironically.*) On the subject of racing-glasses?

FATHER: (*His voice suddenly filled with passion.*) No, Mr Bulstrode. On the subject of love. He told us that he was deeply, sincerely in love with this wife.

THONG: I don't know anything about that.

FATHER: Exactly, Mr Thong! You are hardly an expert witness, are you, on the subject of love? May it please you, my Lord, Members of the Jury. Love has driven men and women in the course of history to curious extremes. It tempted Leander to plunge in and swim the raging Hellespont. It led Juliet to feign death and Ophelia to madness. No doubt it complicated the serenity of the Garden of Eden and we are told started the Trojan War: but surely there is no more curious example of the mysterious effects of the passion than the spectacle of Captain Waring of the Royal Engineers, roosted in a tree, complacently viewing the seduction of his beloved through a pair of strong racing-binoculars…

The SON enters.

Is not the whole story, Members of the Jury, an improbable and impertinent tissue of falsehood…?

The SON is lit downstage as in the upstage darkness, the JUDGE, the FATHER and the MOTHER go and the courtroom furniture is moved away.

SON: (*To the audience.*) He sent words out into the darkness, like soldiers sent off to battle, and was never short of reinforcements. In the Law Courts he gave his public performance. At home he returned to his ritual of the potting shed, the crossword puzzle and, when I was at home, the afternoon walk. The woods were dark and full of flies and we used to pick bracken leaves to swat them, and when I was a child he told me that we carried cutlasses to hack our way through the jungle. I used to shut my eyes at dead rats, or magpies gibbeted on the trees: sights his blindness spared him. He used to walk with his hand on my arm. A small hand, with loose brown skin. From time to time, I had the urge to pull away, to run and hide among the trees...to leave him alone, lost in perpetual darkness. But then his hand would tighten on my sleeve; he was very persistent...

The FATHER enters, takes the SON's arm, and they walk round slowly.

The lights come up.

FATHER: I've had a good deal of fun – out of the Law.

SON: Have you ever been to the South of France?

FATHER: Once or twice... It's all right, except for the dreadful greasy food they can't stop talking about.

SON: Bill and Daphne say the worst of the War is that they can't get to the South of France.

FATHER: Who're they?

SON: The ladies from the bookshop.

FATHER: The ones who downed all our sherry?

SON: That's right.

47

FATHER: My heart bled for you on that occasion.

SON: Daphne's Miss Cox.

FATHER: And Bill?

SON: Bill's Miss Baker.

FATHER: Damned rum!

SON: They practically lived in Cannes before the War. They met Cocteau…

FATHER: Who?

SON: He smoked opium. Have you ever smoked opium?

FATHER: Certainly not! Gives you constipation. Dreadful binding effect. Ever seen those pictures of the wretched poet Coleridge? Green around the gills. And a stranger to the lavatory. Avoid opium.

SON: They may find me a war job.

FATHER: Who may?

SON: Miss Baker and Miss Cox.

FATHER: Why, is old 'Bill' on the General Staff?

SON: They have a friend who makes propaganda films for the government. He needs an assistant.

FATHER: You're thinking of entering the film world?

SON: Just – for the duration.

FATHER: Well! At least there's nothing heroic about it.

SON: No.

FATHER: Rum sort of world, isn't it – the film world?

SON: I expect so.

FATHER: Don't they wear their caps *back to front* in the film world?

SON: You're thinking of the silent days.

FATHER: Am I? I expect I am. Your Mother and I went to a silent film once. In Glastonbury.

SON: Did you?

FATHER: Yes. We were staying there in a hotel. Damn dull. Nothing to do in the evenings. So we sallied forth, to see this silent film. The point was, I invariably dressed for dinner, when in Glastonbury. Follow?

SON: I follow.

FATHER: And when we entered this picture palace
– in evening dress, the audience burst into spontaneous applause! I believe they took us, for part of the entertainment! Rum kind of world, I must say. Now where are we?

SON: At the bottom of Stonor Hill.

FATHER: Good. I'll rest a moment. Then we'll go up to the top.

The SON moves him to the right part of the platform and sits him down.

SON: Will we?

FATHER: Of course we will! You can see three counties from the top of Stonor Hill. Don't you want to see three counties…?

SON: All right.

FATHER: See everything. Everything in Nature… That's the instinct of the May Beetle. Twenty-four hours to live, so spend it – looking around.

SON: We've got more time…

FATHER: Don't you believe it! It's short – but enjoyable! You know what?

SON: What?

FATHER: If they ever say to you, 'Your old father, he couldn't have enjoyed life much. Overdrawn at the bank and bad-tempered and people didn't often visit him…' 'Nonsense,' you can say. 'He enjoyed every minute of it…'

SON: Do you want to go on now?

FATHER: When you consider the embryo of the liver-fluke, born in sheep's droppings, searching the world for a shell to bore into for the sake of living in a snail until it becomes tadpole-like and leaves its host – only to be swallowed up by a sheep again! When you consider that – complicated persistence, well, of course, I've clung on for sixty-five years. It's the instinct – that's all. The irresistible instinct! All right. We'll go up. Watch carefully and you'll see three counties…

The FATHER puts out his hand. The SON pulls him up and they go off.

The lights change.

MISS BAKER and MISS COX enter, carrying a picnic basket and a bird in a large cage. They settle down to a picnic.

MISS COX: Our last picnic…

MISS BAKER: Oh, for God's sake, Daphne. I mean they're not sending me to the Western Desert. Now, let's find a bit of shade for Miss Garbo.

She finds a place for the bird.

MISS COX: Did we have to bring her?

MISS BAKER: She likes the air here. Up Stonor Hill. Where's the sandwiches? Thanks.

MISS COX: (*Putting out sandwiches sadly.*) I know you will…

MISS BAKER: You know I will what? (*Gives a bit of sandwich to the bird.*) Do you know this bloody bird gets all my butter ration.

MISS COX: Fall for some carrot-haired number – with dung all over her jods.

MISS BAKER: Why should I?

MISS COX: She'll be washing you down in the evenings. In front of the fire.

MISS BAKER: I'm not going down the mines either!

MISS COX: I know. (*Half laughing, half starting to cry.*) It's going to be bloody lonely.

MISS BAKER: Cheer up, old thing. Keep smiling.

They lie together, MISS BAKER feeding MISS COX with the remains of her sandwich.

The FATHER and SON enter.

FATHER: What can you see?

SON: Three counties…

FATHER: Be my eyes then. Paint me the picture.

SON: (*After a pause.*) I can just see three counties. Stretched out. That's all I can see.

FATHER: A fine prospect?

SON: A fine prospect.

FATHER: We've bagged a good many sights today! What've we seen?

SON: We saw that hare. Oh, and the butterfly.

FATHER: Danaies Chrysippus! The one that flaunts a large type of powder-puff. You described it to me.

SON: Shall we go home now?

FATHER: You painted me the picture. (*After a pause.*) We've seen a lot today. We've seen a good deal of the monstrous persistence of Nature…

The FATHER and SON move away upstage. MISS BAKER takes her hand off MISS COX's mouth, releasing a cascade of giggles, as –

the Curtain falls.

Act Two

As the curtain rises, there is the noise of carpentry, shouting, singing and cursing. SPARKS is sitting on a chair with his feet on the table. The TECHNICIANS enter bringing a movie camera on a tripod, a microphone on a pole, a case of make-up and a typewriter. The DIRECTOR is smoking a Wills Whiff. The Unit Manager, DORIS, is carrying a clipboard and is a tough, competent, deep-voiced woman.

DORIS: Move over, Sparks.

SPARKS: (*Singing loudly.*) 'Oh Salome, Salome,
        That's my girl, Salome.
        Standing there with her arse all bare…'

DORIS: (*Yelling.*) Let's have a little quiet, please!

SPARKS: (*Singing quietly.*) 'Every little wrinkle makes the boys all stare…'

DORIS: (*In a full-throated roar.*) Great Scott, Sparks!

SPARKS: Sorry, Doris.

DORIS: You the new assistant?

SON: Yes.

DORIS: Know your job do you?

SON: I'm new to movies.

DORIS: Great Scott! You don't have to know anything about movies! You're here to fetch the subsistence…

SON: The what?

DORIS: Tea breaks. Coffee breaks. After-lunch-special breaks and in-lieu-of-breakfast breaks. The Sparks have tea and ham and lettuce rolls, known to them as Smiggett sandwiches. The Chippies take coffee and cakes with coconut icing. The director needs Horlicks, liver pâté sandwiches and Wills Whiffs. Keep your mouth shut except to call in a firm and authoritative tone for 'quiet' when we shoot. Any questions?

SON: Yes.

DORIS: What?

SON: Where do I get liver pâté sandwiches?

DORIS: Use your bloody imagination! That's what you came into the film business for…

DIRECTOR: (*Calling her from the camera.*) Doris!

DORIS: Coming, Humphrey. (*To the SON.*) Next tea break in ten minutes.

She goes to chatter to the DIRECTOR.

The SON runs downstage. SPARKS shouts after him.

SPARKS: Hey! You lost something?

SON: Well, actually I'm…

SPARKS: Don't worry. Maybe you left it in the Officer's Mess. You know we've got two ATS in the next scene don't you?

SON: No I didn't.

SPARKS: There's two sorts of ATS let me tell you. Cocked ATS and felt ATS. Had it in last night, did you?

Two ATS enter.

SON: I beg your pardon?

SPARKS: Seen the King last night?

SON: The King? No. (*Innocently.*) Was he here?

SPARKS: Was he here? That's a good one. Who did you say you was out with?

SON: Actually, no one.

SPARKS: Didn't spend out on her I hope? Never spend out 'til you've had it in. Then you can buy her a packet of small smokes.

DIRECTOR: All right, we'll try a rehearsal.

DORIS: Stand by!

SPARKS: What did you say you was looking for?

SON: A liver pâté sandwich.

SPARKS: Liver pâté! You're a caution! That's what you are.

DORIS: Rehearsal!

SPARKS: Lights, Alf!

DIRECTOR: All right, then. Settle down…and – action.

FIRST ATS: Gerry's being a bit naughty tonight then, Hilda.

SECOND ATS: Yes. (*She offers the other a cup of tea.*) Tea, luv?

FIRST ATS: Ta, luv.

SECOND ATS: Sugars, do you?

FIRST ATS: Ta.

SECOND ATS: One or two sugars?

FIRST ATS: Two sugars, ta. (*After a pause.*) Ta.

SECOND ATS: (*After a pause.*) You know, I've been thinking lately.

FIRST ATS: Have you, Hilda?

SECOND ATS: Oh, yes, Sandra, I've been thinking.

FIRST ATS: What about then, Hilda?

SECOND ATS: You know what I reckon this war's all about?

FIRST ATS: (*After a long pause.*) No.

SECOND ATS: It's just our freedom. To talk to each other.

FIRST ATS: Sugar for you then Hilda? You want sugar, luv?

DIRECTOR: Cut! That was marvellous. Tremendously real.

SPARKS: Save the lights, Alf!

The lights change.

DIRECTOR: My God, you couldn't do that with actors! All right, Doris. I'm going for a take.

DORIS: Assistant! Get a bit of silence, will you?

SON: (*Turning away from the tea-tray.*) Sorry, Doris.

DORIS: Yell 'quiet', for God's sake.

SON: (*Moving to the centre of the stage and clearing his throat nervously.*) Quiet, please!

The noise of the unit continues.

Can we have a little quiet now, please?

From this moment the noise intensifies. The two ATS start to dance together, humming 'The White Cliffs of Dover'.

We'd appreciate a bit of quiet now, thank you!

Noise.

All quiet now! We're going to try a take.

Noise.

Ladies and gentlemen, will you please give us a little *quiet*!

Noise.

Quiet now, PLEASE!

There is increased noise.

(*Becoming hysterical and yelling.*) SHUT UP, YOU BASTARDS!

SPARKS: All out!

Total silence.

SON: No, please.

ELIZABETH enters with a typewriter, sits at the table and starts to type. All except ELIZABETH and SON exit, with equipment.

(Moving towards ELIZABETH.) Is this the writers' department?

The typing continues.

They say I'm not cut out by nature to be an Assistant Director. When I yelled for 'quiet' all the electricians went on strike.

The typing continues.

They say with me as an Assistant Director the War'd be over before they finished the movie.

She stops typing, looks up at him and smiles for the first time. Encouraged, he goes and looks at what she is typing.

What's the script?

ELIZABETH: It's something Humphrey wants to do. *(She pulls a face.)* There's a character in it called the 'Common Man'. He keeps on saying, 'Look here, matey, what is the World Health Organization?'

SON: Sounds ghastly.

ELIZABETH: *(Smiling slightly.)* Yes, it is rather.

SON: Why on earth do you bother to write it?

ELIZABETH: I suppose – the school fees.

SON: Oh, you're studying something?

ELIZABETH: No, you fool. It's my kids. Peter's only got his captain's pay and I can't…

SON: Peter?

ELIZABETH: My husband.

SON: He's overseas?

ELIZABETH: Uxbridge. In Army education.

SON: My father says that in time of war one should avoid the temptation to do anything heroic.

ELIZABETH: How odd.

SON: What?

ELIZABETH: Odd thing for him to say.

SON: You know, I think after today I'll abandon the film business and take up the Law. My father's a lawyer.

ELIZABETH: Do you always copy your father?

SON: Good God, no!

ELIZABETH: Really? You look the type to agree with Dad.

SON: (*Looking at her.*) Well, there's one thing he says I don't agree with at all.

ELIZABETH: What's that?

SON: He says that sex has been greatly overrated. By the poets...

The SON goes. The DIRECTOR enters as the rest of the film unit clear the film gear from the stage.

DIRECTOR: Is he going to be of any use to you, Elizabeth?

ELIZABETH: Who?

DIRECTOR: Our new writer.

ELIZABETH: Oh, I shouldn't think so. Is he going to stay?

DIRECTOR: (*Reading.*) What?

ELIZABETH: Just passing through. That's the feeling I get about him.

The DIRECTOR and ELIZABETH go.

The lights change.

The FATHER enters half-dressed, without his coat, waistcoat or tie. He hooks his braces over his shoulders, shouts, moves round the stage, his hands out in front of him, groping for the furniture that is not there.

FATHER: My tie. Oh, God in heaven, where's my tie? Will no one bring me a waistcoat even? Can't any of you realize the loneliness of getting dressed?

The SON enters with the coat, waistcoat and tie over his arm, finds the FATHER's wandering hand and puts the tie into it.

Is that you?

SON: Yes. It's me.

FATHER: I suppose you expect me to talk about it.

SON: I know it came as a bit of a shock to you, when Peter divorced Elizabeth.

FATHER: Must have come as a shock to you, too, didn't it? The fact that she was available for marriage must have somewhat cooled your ardour. I mean you're hardly in a state to get married...

SON: Do you want to stop us?

FATHER: Are you asking me to?

SON: Of course not.

FATHER: How long have you been at the bar, exactly?

SON: Nine months.

FATHER: Nine months! I'd been in practice for ten years before I felt the slightest need to marry your mother.

SON: Perhaps – needs weren't so urgent then.

FATHER: Got any work to do?

SON: A little work.

FATHER: Unsuccessful defence in serious case of non-renewed dog licence. That'll hardly keep you in Vim...

SON: But we don't want to be kept in Vim.

FATHER: But you'll have no alternative – once you're married. Your no-income will be frittered away on Vim, saucepans, scourers, Mansion polish, children's vests and such-like luxuries...

SON: I'm quite prepared to take on her children.

FATHER: You sound like a railway train. Short stop to take on children. Waistcoat anywhere about?

SON: Wait.

FATHER: Yes. In the course of her life – she has acquired children. Mixed blessings I should imagine, for both of you.

SON: If you're worried about money...

FATHER: My dear boy. I'm not worried about it. I just think you haven't bargained for the Vim. Now how long are you going to deny me my waistcoat?

SON: Oh, here.

The SON holds out the waistcoat, helps the FATHER to struggle into it.

I know you think we're insane...

FATHER: (*Buttoning his waistcoat.*) You feel the need to be dissuaded.

SON: Of course not.

FATHER: I can't help you, you know.

SON: We don't want help.

FATHER: From what I hear, the children seem quite lively. As children go.

SON: Coat.

FATHER: Of course it won't be I, who has to keep them in rompers, I wonder, should I have a drop of eau-de-Cologne on the handkerchief? I understand your poor girl's coming to tea. We seem nowadays to be totally surrounded by visitors.

SON: You're not going to be rude to her?

FATHER: No, of course not! Your poor girl and I have got a certain understanding…

SON: For God's sake. Why do you keep calling her my poor girl?

FATHER: That's something – I'll have to explain to her after tea.

The FATHER takes the SON's arm. They move off the stage together. ELIZABETH enters. She waits nervously in the garden area: lights a cigarette. The SON enters, goes to her quickly, also nervous.

SON: They're just coming… (*He pauses.*) It's going to be all right. (*He pauses.*) You won't mind, whatever he says?

ELIZABETH: Will you?

SON: No. Of course not.

ELIZABETH: *Whatever* he says?

SON: I'm used to it. (*He pauses.*) He doesn't mean half of it.

ELIZABETH: Yes, I know. But it's difficult…

SON: What?

ELIZABETH: Telling which half he means.

The FATHER enters in his garden hat, his hand on the MOTHER's arm.

FATHER: Rhododendrons out?

MOTHER: Yes, dear.

FATHER: A fine show of rhododendrons. And the little syringa?

MOTHER: Just out.

FATHER: Just out. And smelling sweetly. Azaleas doing well?

MOTHER: Well, we can see they're a little brown, round the edges…

FATHER: Azaleas doing moderately well. Is our visitor here?

MOTHER: Yes, dear. Elizabeth's here.

SON: We're both here.

FATHER: And is your visitor enjoying the garden?

ELIZABETH: Very much. Thank you.

FATHER: Good. And is he treating you well?

ELIZABETH: Quite well. Thank you.

FATHER: I've often wondered about my son. Does he treat girls well…?

SON: Why've you wondered that?

FATHER: Well, I once knew a man named Arthur Pennycuick. Like you in some ways. He didn't treat girls well…

MOTHER: Please, dear – Arthur Pennycuick's not quite suitable.

ELIZABETH: Tell us. What did he do to girls?

FATHER: When I was a young man, I was out with this Pennycuick. And he picked up a girl. In the promenade of the old Alhambra Music-Hall. And just before he went off

62

with her, he took out his cuff-links and handed them to me for safe keeping. In her presence! I was so sick and angry, seeing him take out his old gold cuff-links. I never spoke to him again. Disgusting!

ELIZABETH: You think if you sleep with someone – you should trust them with your cuff-links?

FATHER: At least not take them out – *in front of the girl*! Well, we can see a fine show of rhododendrons.

MOTHER: Yes, dear. And I showed you the polyanthus.

FATHER: A reward at last, for a good deal of tedious potting up.

ELIZABETH: Why do you bother?

FATHER: About what?

ELIZABETH: I said why do you bother to do all this gardening? I mean when you can't see it…

The SON tries to interrupt her protectively.

SON: Elizabeth…

ELIZABETH: Well, he can't, can he? Why do you all walk about – pretending he's not blind?

The FATHER moves, his hand out in front of him, towards ELIZABETH. He gets to her: touches her arm, feels down her arm, and puts his in it.

FATHER: Is this you?

ELIZABETH: Yes…

FATHER: Would you take me to West Copse? I'd like a report on the magnolia. Would you do that? (*He pauses.*) Be my eyes.

ELIZABETH: Come then…

She moves away, with the FATHER on her arm.

MOTHER: (*Looking after ELIZABETH.*) She has nice eyes.

SON: Yes.

MOTHER: Not at all the eyes of a divorced person.

SON: (*After a pause.*) Does he want to stop us?

MOTHER: Well, it's not easy for him. He's such a household word in the Probate, Divorce and Admiralty Division.

SON: Is he going on about that?

MOTHER: No, no, not at all.

SON: If he could only see her he'd understand why I want to marry her.

MOTHER: Oh, he understands that. I think his main difficulty is understanding why she wants to marry you...

SON: (*Gives a half laugh.*) Nice of him!

MOTHER: Would you like to come and help me cut up the oranges? I do so hate making marmalade.

The MOTHER exits.

SON: (*Shouts after her.*) For God's sake, why don't you buy it?

SON exits downstage. FATHER and ELIZABETH enter upstage.

FATHER: Come over, did you, in your own small car?

ELIZABETH: You've been trying to put him off.

FATHER: Not at all.

ELIZABETH: I told him. You'd put him off.

FATHER: He came to me for advice.

ELIZABETH: And I suppose you gave it.

FATHER: I never give advice. Bit of an asset, don't you find it, that private transport?

ELIZABETH: We've made up our minds.

64

FATHER: And I believe your children are quite lively. For children...

ELIZABETH: He gets on marvellously with them...

FATHER: And I believe you have your own bits and pieces of furniture. A bedroom suite they tell me. In a fine state of preservation. You're a catch! If you want my honest opinion.

ELIZABETH: Well, then you ought to be glad for him...

FATHER: For him? Look here. Joking apart. You don't want to marry him, do you? I mean he's got no assets – of any kind. Not even – a kitchen cabinet. And here's another thing about it. He won't like it, you know. If you get the flu...

ELIZABETH: Really...?

FATHER: Most people are sympathetic towards illness. They're kind to people with high temperatures. They even cosset them. But not him! Sneeze once and he'll be off! In the opposite direction!

ELIZABETH: I don't get ill all that much...

FATHER: Well, if you do – he'll run a mile!

ELIZABETH: I thought it was *me* you might disapprove of...

FATHER: Why ever...?

ELIZABETH: Think he's marrying someone unsuitable...

FATHER: You have particularly nice eyes they tell me.

ELIZABETH: Thank you.

FATHER: And your own bits and pieces of furniture...

ELIZABETH: Not much.

FATHER: And as you told me yourself, your own small runabout.

ELIZABETH: Very bashed.

FATHER: All the same. Not many girls with assets of that description. Couldn't you do better, than someone who bolts if you go two ticks above normal?

ELIZABETH: Well, I hadn't thought about it.

FATHER: Oh, do think. Think carefully! There must be bigger fish than *that* in your own particular sea. You are, I mean, something of a catch. You could catch better fish than *that*. I'm prepared to take a bet on it…

(He shivers slightly.) It's getting cold.

ELIZABETH: *(Unsmiling.)* I'll take you in.

The FATHER gets up and ELIZABETH leads him off the stage. The SON enters, wearing a black coat and striped trousers.

SON: *(To the audience.)* In that case his advocacy failed. In time he became reconciled to me as a husband for his daughter-in-law.

GEORGE enters. He is on is way home.

Any work for me tomorrow in court, George?

GEORGE: Come now, sir. We were in court last week. We mustn't be greedy.

SON: No. I suppose not. Good night, George. Don't work too hard.

GEORGE goes and ELIZABETH enters.

(To the audience.) My father was right, though. I hadn't bargained for the Vim.

ELIZABETH: Made lots of money this week?

SON: Ten guineas. For a divorce.

ELIZABETH: That's marvellous, darling! I had to get them new vests.

SON: What in the hell do they do with their vests? You know, it's my opinion they eat their vests.

ELIZABETH: And kicker linings. I put them on the account at John Barnes.

SON: The account at John Barnes is assuming the proportions of the national debt.

ELIZABETH: You ought to be rich.

SON: Ought?

ELIZABETH: I am up all night. Typing your divorce petitions. They must be paying you – for all those paragraphs of deep humiliation and distress.

SON: You don't get paid for years. In the Law.

ELIZABETH: Can't you ask for it?

SON: Of course you can't.

ELIZABETH: Why not?

SON: You just can't knock on someone's door and say, 'Can I have ten guineas for the divorce.'

ELIZABETH: I'll go and knock if you like...

SON: Anyway George collects the fees...

ELIZABETH: Who's George?

SON: Our clerk. It's his department.

ELIZABETH: I thought his name was Henry.

SON: It is but my father calls him George.

ELIZABETH: Whatever for?

SON: Because he once had a clerk called George, who was killed on the Somme. So when Henry took over my father continued to call him George.

ELIZABETH: Well, Henry doesn't much like that, if you ask me.

SON: He doesn't mind.

ELIZABETH: You always think no one minds – about your father…

SON: Let's go to the pub.

ELIZABETH: What on?

SON: The Family Allowance.

ELIZABETH: All right. Shall we play bar billiards?

SON: Like that night when Peter walked in. Remember?

ELIZABETH: And said, 'This is the end of our marriage. I see you have become entirely trivial.'

SON: Do you miss Peter?

ELIZABETH: No. Do you?

SON: No. (*After a pause.*) Of course not!

ELIZABETH: I'm sorry.

SON: What about?

ELIZABETH: About John Barnes.

SON: That's marriage.

ELIZABETH: What's marriage?

SON: An unexpectedly large expenditure on Vim, children's vests and such-like luxuries…

ELIZABETH smiles knowingly at him.

ELIZABETH: And who's that quotation from?

ELIZABETH exits. GEORGE enters, sits silently at the table, and dozes off. The SON crosses to him, leans over, opens his drawer and takes out a cheque.

GEORGE: We have been going, sir, to our personal drawer!

SON: But, George, it's a cheque, for me...

GEORGE: We should have given it out to us, sir, in the fullness of time...

SON: Fifteen guineas! Thank God for adultery.

GEORGE: We have never had a gentleman here in chambers, sir, that had to grub for money in our personal top drawer...

SON: But, George, we're desperately short of Vim.

GEORGE: These things take time.

SON: And what's the point of keeping good money shut up with a box of old pen nibs and a Lyons Individual Fruit Pie. I mean, what's it meant to do in there – breed or something? Don't look at me like that, George. If only you could get me some more work.

GEORGE: We can't expect much. We must wait until a few clients learn to like the cut of our jib.

SON: I have a talent for divorcing people.

GEORGE: It's not our work. It's our conversation to solicitors that counts. While we're waiting to come on, at London Sessions.

SON: Conversations?

GEORGE: Do we ask about their tomato plants? Do we remember ourselves to their motor mowers? Do we show a proper concern for their operations and their daughters' figure-skating? That's how we rise to heights in the Law.

SON: My father doesn't do that.

GEORGE: Your father's a case apart.

SON: (*Rather proud.*) My father's obnoxious, to solicitors.

GEORGE: (*Suddenly shouts.*) 'The devil damn thee Black, thou cream-faced loon!'

SON: (*Taken aback.*) George!

GEORGE: He said that to Mr Binns, when he'd forgotten to file his affidavit. Yes. Your father is something of an exception.

SON: Yes.

GEORGE: I sometimes wonder. Does he realize I'm one of the many Henrys of the world?

SON: (*Reassuringly.*) I'm sure he does, George.

GEORGE looks at the SON more sympathetically. There is a pause.

GEORGE: Mr Garfield goes down to the Free Legal Centre, Holloway Road. That's where he goes of a Thursday. He picks up the odd guinea or two, or poor persons' cases. And I don't have him in here, sir, ferreting about among my packed meal, sir.

SON: Mr Garfield lives with his mother – he spends nothing at all on Vim!

GEORGE: He takes the view he might rise to fame from the Free Legal Centre. He says a murderer might rush in there off the streets any day of the week...

The lights change. The SON moves forward and speaks to the audience.

GEORGE exits. A table, chair and portrait of George VI is set. MISS FERGUSON, a social worker with glasses, chain-smoking over a pile of files, enters.

SON: So I went to the Free Legal Centre and I waited in a small room which smelt of gym shoes and coconut matting and I used to pray that a murderer, still clutching the dripping knife, might burst in from the Holloway Road

70

begging urgently for Legal Aid. Any murderers for me tonight, Miss Ferguson?

MISS FERGUSON: I'm just away to send you in my Mr Morrow. I chose you out for him specially.

SON: Why me?

MISS FERGUSON: He makes Mr Garfield faint. Mr Morrow!

MISS FERGUSON exits. MR MORROW enters.

MR MORROW: You the lawyer?

SON: Mr Morrow? Is it matrimonial?

MR MORROW: Yes, sir. In a sense...

SON: Now, you were married on...?

MR MORROW: The sixth day of month one. I prefer not to use heathen notation.

SON: Nineteen-forty?

MR MORROW: Nineteen-forty.

SON: I have to write it down on this form, you see. (*He pauses.*) Now, what is the trouble?

MR MORROW: The corpuscles.

SON: But there's no place on the free legal form for corpuscles.

MR MORROW: Which is, however, the trouble. That's what I want, sir. The legal position... She's on to the red ones now. I could just about stand it when she only took the white. And my child, sir. My Pamela. I have a very particular respect for that child, sir, who is now losing her hearty appetite.

SON: What is your wife doing, exactly?

MR MORROW: She is eating our red corpuscles.

SON: Mr Morrow, if you're not feeling well...

71

MR MORROW: She drains them from us, by the use of her specs, sir. That is how she drains them out. She focuses her rimless specs upon our bodies, and so our bodies bleed.

SON: Mr Morrow...

MR MORROW: I was standing upon my hearthrug, sir, which lies upon my hearth. I looked down and I saw it there. The scarlet flower. There was the stain of blood all over my white fleecy rug, sir.

SON: Have you spoken to your wife about this at all?

MR MORROW: I haven't spoken to her, sir. But she is forgiven. All the same I feel she has let me down. When it was only the white she focused her eyes on, it was more or less immaterial. But now she's after my vital strength.

SON: But you see, legally – there's not a great deal I...

MR MORROW: A man stands entitled to his own blood, sir, surely. It must be so.

SON: I know of no case decided on this particular issue.

MR MORROW: So you're advising me to go to Doncaster?

SON: You might as well.

MR MORROW: It's your considered and expert opinion, her destructive eye won't be on me in Doncaster?

SON: Why not give it a try, anyway?

MR MORROW: Very well, sir, I will. I bow to your honest opinion. I shall discontinue all legal proceedings and proceed at once to Doncaster. Will you require my signature to that effect?

SON: Well, no, I hardly think so.

MR MORROW: That's just as well, as it so happens. I never sign – ethical reasons.

MR MORROW exits. MISS FERGUSON enters.

MISS FERGUSON: Oh uhhu. Mr Morrow looks well contented.

SON: He should. He has absolutely no need of the Law.

MISS FERGUSON exits. The FATHER enters.

FATHER: 'Let's talk of graves of worms and epitaphs.'

SON: Back in chambers my father, smelling of eau-de-Cologne and occasional cigars, sat among his relics, the blown duck egg on which a client's will had once been written, the caricatures of himself in famous cases. He wrote a great textbook on the law of wills, becoming expert in the habits of mad old ladies who went fishing for gold under their beds and left all their money to undesirable causes.

FATHER: 'Let's choose executors and talk of wills.
         And yet not so… For what can we bequeath?
         Save our deposed bodies to the ground.
         Our lands, our lives and all are Bolingbroke's.
         And nothing can we call our own but death
         And that small model of the barren earth…
         Which serves as paste and cover to our bones.'

   You're back from lunch.

SON: Yes.

FATHER: You took a long time.

SON: I went to see a man – who might want to put on my play…

FATHER: Possibly you would work harder if you were a woman barrister.

SON: Possibly…

FATHER: I've often said to George, 'Why don't we have a woman in chambers?' Women work so much harder than men. They can be imposed on so much more easily. Look how seriously girls' schools take lacrosse! They'd treat the

Law like that. I could get a ridiculous amount of work from a woman pupil.

SON: What does George say?

FATHER: He says there's not the toilet facilities. Enjoying the Law, are you?

SON: Not all that much.

FATHER: Plays are all very well. Photographs in the paper may be very fine and large. But you need something real! Hold hard on the Law.

SON: Are you sure the Law's real?

FATHER: What on earth do you mean?

SON: No one seems to need it – except lawyers...

FATHER: The Law's not designed for imbeciles, or for your friends who combine the art of being called Bill with membership of the female sex. It's not exactly tailor-made for the poet Percy Bysshe Shelley. No! The whole point of the Law is – it's designed for the ordinary everyday citizen seated aboard the ordinary, everyday Holborn tramcar.

SON: I don't think they have tramcars in Holborn any more.

FATHER: That's hardly the point.

SON: No tramcars and no ordinary common-sense citizens sitting on them. No. They're all busy thinking about the things that really worry them, like the shapes on the ceilings and the stains on the carpet, and, do you know, they only pretend to be ordinary common-sense citizens when they need lawyers. It's a disguise they put on, like the blue suit and the old Boy Scout button, and the pathetic voices they use when they take the Bible oath. They're fooling us, that's what they're doing. Because they think if they play our game we'll let them off their debts, or we'll order their wives to permit them sexual intercourse, or we'll liberate them from old pointless crimes no one holds against them anyway. No, honestly, all this legal language we're so proud of, it might just as well be Chinese...

FATHER: (*Conciliating.*) Oh, come now, I mean – you can get a lot of innocent fun out of the Law. How's your cross?

SON: What?

FATHER: Your cross-examination. In court – have you the makings of a cross-examiner?

SON: I don't know.

FATHER: Timing is of great importance. In the art of cross-examination.

SON: That's show business.

FATHER: How do you mean?

SON: It's an expression, used by actors.

FATHER: (*Without interest.*) Really? How very uninteresting. Now I always count, in silence of course, up to forty-three before starting a cross-examination.

SON: Whatever for?

FATHER: The witness imagines you're thinking up some utterly devastating question.

SON: Are you?

FATHER: Of course not. I'm just counting. Up to forty-three. But, it unnerves the gentleman in the box. Then, start off with the knock-out! Don't leave it 'til the end: go in with your guns blazing! Ask him...

SON: What?

FATHER: Is there anything in your conduct, Mr Nokes, of which, looking back on it, you feel you are now heartily *ashamed*?

SON: Is that a good question?

FATHER: It's an excellent question!

SON: Why exactly?

FATHER: Because if he says 'yes' he's made an admission,
and if he says 'no' he's a self-satisfied idiot and he's lost the
sympathy of the court.

SON: Anything else?

FATHER: Suppose you have a letter from him in which
he admits something discreditable – like, well, having
apologized to his wife for instance. Now then, how're you
going to put that to him?

SON: Did you, or did you not –

FATHER: Not bad.

SON: – write a letter apologizing to your wife?

FATHER: Well, I suppose you're young.

SON: Isn't that right?

FATHER: Not what I'd call the *art* of cross-examination.

SON: Then how…?

FATHER: You be Nokes.

SON: Right.

FATHER: You behaved disgracefully to your wife, did you not?

SON: No.

FATHER: In fact, so disgracefully that you had to apologize to
her.

SON: I don't remember.

FATHER: Will you swear you did not?

SON: What?

FATHER: Will you swear you didn't apologize to her?

SON: All right.

FATHER: Now just turn to the letter on page twenty-three. Just read it out to us, will you?

SON: I see. (*He pauses.*) But what's the point of all this, actually?

FATHER: (*Standing up; very positive.*) The point? My dear boy, the point is to down your opponent. To obliterate whoever's agin you. That's what the point of it is... And, of course, to have a little fun, while you're about it.

Tapping with his stick, the FATHER feels his way off. The SON moves downstage and speaks to the audience.

SON: My father got too old for the train journey to London...

A ROBING-ROOM MAN comes in with a wig and gown, stand-up collar and bands; and stands by the SON. As he speaks the SON unfixes his own collar, hands it to the man and takes the collar which is handed to him and puts it on, ties the bands and is robed in the wig and gown. A JUDGE is sitting in wig and gown. A Lady WITNESS, in a flowered hat and gloves, is waiting to be questioned.

My father retired on a pension of nothing but credit, optimism and the determination not to think of anything unpleasant. His money had gone on cigars and barrels of oysters and eau-de-Cologne for his handkerchief and always first class on the railway and great, huge Japanese cherry trees which flowered for two weeks a year in a green-white shower he never saw. He left me all the subtle pleasures of the Law...

JUDGE: (*Loudly to the SON.*) Do you want to cross-examine this witness?

SON: (*Turns round as if woken from a reverie and enters the courtroom scene.*) Most certainly, my Lord.

JUDGE: Very well, get on with it.

SON: (*Turning to the WITNESS.*) Now, madam...

WITNESS: Yes.

SON: (*Starting to count under his breath.*) One – two – three
– four – five – six – seven…

JUDGE: Are you intending to ask any questions?

SON: I'm sorry, my Lord?

JUDGE: If you have a question to ask, ask it. We can't all wait
while you stand in silent prayer, you know.

SON: Now, madam. Is there anything in your conduct of
which, looking back on it, you now feel heartily ashamed?

WITNESS: (*After a pause.*) Yes.

SON: Ah. And what are you ashamed of?

WITNESS: Well, I once wrote up for an autograph – with
picture. You know the type of thing. At my age! Well, I
began off, 'Am heartily ashamed to write up but…'

JUDGE: Have you any relevant questions?

SON: Now, madam, would you be so kind as to read this
letter? – which I am about to hand you.

WITNESS: Oh, yes. Thank you.

SON: Will you please read it out to us, please, madam.

WITNESS: I can't…

SON: Madam. The court is waiting…

WITNESS: I really can't.

SON: Is there something in that letter which you would rather
not remember?

WITNESS: No. Not exactly…

SON: (*Very severely.*) Then read it to us, madam!

WITNESS: Then, could I borrow your glasses?

All on stage except the SON, laugh.

SON: It was years before it got any better.

The members of the court exit, removing and replacing the courtroom furniture.

But then quite suddenly all the judges seemed to get younger. I forgot my father's timing, and I began to enjoy a modest success.

The SON exits. The FATHER enters, then the MOTHER. The FATHER carries a newspaper.

FATHER: Elizabeth?

MOTHER: No.

ELIZABETH enters.

They're giving him a lot of briefs.

ELIZABETH: Yes.

MOTHER: It's hard to believe. Of course his father would so have enjoyed Clarkson v. Clarkson.

ELIZABETH: Oh, yes, I'm sure he would.

MOTHER: It must be keeping you very busy.

ELIZABETH: Me? Why me?

MOTHER: Don't you help him with his cases?

ELIZABETH: Oh, he's got a secretary now. He hardly ever discusses his work: he thinks I take it too seriously.

MOTHER: Of course his father misses going to London. He used to get such a lot of fun, out of the divorce cases.

FATHER: (*Opening his eyes.*) What's that?

MOTHER: I said you missed going to London, dear.

FATHER: It's my son, you know. He's pinched all my work. Are we still waiting?

MOTHER: Yes, dear, we're still waiting. Children all settled?

ELIZABETH: Yes, they're all settled.

MOTHER: And how's our little Jennifer?

ELIZABETH: Your little Jennifer's fine, and the same goes for our little Daniel and Jonathan.

MOTHER: Jenny's so pretty. I'd like to have done a drawing of her. Perhaps a pastel.

ELIZABETH: Well, why don't you?

MOTHER: Oh, I gave up drawing when I got married. You have to, don't you – give up things when you get married…

ELIZABETH: Do you?

MOTHER: Of course now there's no time…

ELIZABETH: (*Looking at the FATHER and whispering.*) Doesn't he ever leave you half an hour to yourself?

MOTHER: He doesn't like to be left. I suppose I often think. Some day I'll be alone, shan't I. You can't help thinking.

ELIZABETH: What'll you do? Travel. Go to France.

MOTHER: Well, I shan't dig the garden for one thing.

The SON enters with a tray of Champagne and glasses.

SON: (*Pause.*) The traffic was Hell!

ELIZABETH: What happened, darling?

SON: I won – Clarkson v. Clarkson, after five days.

FATHER: (*Smacking his lips.*) Five refreshers!

SON: They insisted on fighting every inch of the way. Terribly litigious…

FATHER: The sort to breed from – those Clarksons!

SON: I brought Champagne…

MOTHER: Oh, how festive.

SON: For a small celebration.

ELIZABETH: (*Muttering.*) Just like a wedding.

SON: What did you say?

ELIZABETH: Nothing.

MOTHER: Isn't it festive, dear?

FATHER: Festive indeed!

MOTHER: He's offering you a glass of Champagne.

FATHER: I'm glad you can afford such things, dear boy. I suppose you're polite to solicitors?

SON: Occasionally.

FATHER: I could never bring myself… Pity. If I'd gone to dinner with solicitors I might've had something to leave you – beyond my overdraft. I remember after one case, my solicitor said to me, standing on the platform of Temple Station, 'Are you going west, old boy, we might have dinner together?' 'No,' I lied to him, I was so anxious to get away, 'I'm going east.' I ended up with a sandwich in Bethnal Green. It's been my fault… The determination to be alone. You know what'd go very nicely with this Champagne?

MOTHER: What, dear – a dry biscuit?

FATHER: No.

SON: The crossword.

MOTHER: One across. 'The N.C.O. sounds agony.'

FATHER: 'The N.C.O. sounds agony.' How many letters?

MOTHER: Two words – eight and ten.

FATHER: Corporal punishment.

MOTHER: That's very clever!

FATHER: Oh, I have this crossword fellow at my mercy.

The FATHER and MOTHER exit.

ELIZABETH: And you're very clever, too, darling.

SON: Thank you.

ELIZABETH: The only thing is...

SON: What?

ELIZABETH: I thought – I mean in that Clarkson v. Clarkson
– you were for the husband?

SON: Of course I was for the husband.

ELIZABETH: Wasn't he the man who insisted on his wife
tickling the soles of his feet. For hours at a stretch...

SON: Yes, but it was only while they watched television.

ELIZABETH: With a contraption! A foot tickler...?

SON: It was most ingenious actually. The whole thing was
worked out by a system of weights and pulleys. The actual
act was performed by an old pipe-cleaner.

ELIZABETH: Ought he to have won?

SON: (*Correcting her.*) I won.

ELIZABETH: Yes, but ought you...?

SON: The judge said it was part of the wear and tear of
married life.

ELIZABETH: Yes, but how did *they* feel about it. I mean, I
suppose they're still married, aren't they?

SON: They did look a little confused.

ELIZABETH: Perhaps they didn't appreciate the rules of the game…

SON: Oh, I enjoyed it…

ELIZABETH: You enjoy playing games, don't you?

SON: Yes, I do.

ELIZABETH: You know what?

SON: What?

ELIZABETH: (*Quite loudly.*) You get more like him. Every day.

The FATHER and MOTHER enter.

SON: In his old age, my father's chief sport was starting arguments!

FATHER: Music! I can't imagine anyone actually *liking* music. (*He pauses.*) The immortality of the soul! What a boring concept! I can't think of anything worse than living for eternity in some great transcendental hotel, with nothing to do in the evenings – like that place in Glastonbury. (*He pauses.*) What's the time?

MOTHER: Nearly half past nine.

FATHER: Ah! Time's nipping along nicely. (*He pauses.*) Nothing narrows the mind so much as foreign travel. Stay at home. That's the way to see the world.

ELIZABETH: I don't know that that's true.

FATHER: But of course it's true! And I'll tell you something else, Elizabeth. Just between the two of us. There's a lot of sorry stuff in D. H. Lawrence.

ELIZABETH: I don't know about that either.

FATHER: Oh, yes, there is. And a lot of damned dull stuff in old Proust. (*He pauses.*) Did you hear that, Elizabeth? Lot of damned dull stuff in old Proust.

ELIZABETH: Yes. I heard.

FATHER: Well, I'll say one thing for you – you're an improvement on the ones he used to bring home. Girls that would closet themselves in the bathroom for hours on end. And nothing to show for it. None of them lasted long.

ELIZABETH: I wonder why?

FATHER: Yes. I wonder. At least my son's someone to talk to. Most people get damned dull children.

FATHER puts his hand out, feels the SON's hand.

Is that you?

SON: Yes. It's me.

FATHER: That play of yours came across quite well they tell me.

SON: Yes.

A pause.

MOTHER: Would you like a hot drink?

SON: Nothing, thank you.

A pause.

FATHER: I see that other fellow's play got very good reviews. You want to watch out that he doesn't put your nose out of joint. (*He pauses.*) I haven't been sleeping lately. (*He pauses.*) And when I can't sleep, you know, I sometimes like to make a list of all the things I really hate.

MOTHER: Elizabeth, would you like a hot drink?

ELIZABETH: Is it a long list?

FATHER: No. Not very. Soft eggs. Cold plates. Waiting for things. Parsons.

SON: Parsons?

FATHER: Yes. Parsons. On the wireless. If those fellows bore God as much as they bore me, I'm sorry for Him…

ELIZABETH: My father's a parson.

FATHER: I know. (*He pauses.*) 'Nymph, in thy orisons be all my sins remembered.' (*There is a pause. He smacks at the air with his hand.*) Is that a wasp?

MOTHER: Yes. (*She flaps at the wasp.*)

FATHER: What's it doing?

MOTHER: It's going away.

FATHER: After you've been troubled by a wasp, don't you love a fly? (*He pauses.*) Don't the evenings seem terribly long now you're married? Aren't you finding it tremendously tedious? What do you do – have the wireless?

ELIZABETH: We don't get bored, exactly.

SON: We can always fight.

FATHER: You know, I was surprised about that play of yours.

SON: Were you?

FATHER: Yes. When you told us the story of that play, I said, 'Ha. Ha. This is a bit thin. This is rather poor fooling.' Didn't I say that?

MOTHER: Yes, dear.

FATHER: 'This is likely to come very tardy off.' But now it appears to have come across quite well. Didn't that surprise you, Elizabeth?

ELIZABETH: Well…

SON: She doesn't like it.

FATHER: What?

SON: Elizabeth doesn't like it very much.

FATHER: (*Interested.*) Really? That's interesting. Now tell me why…

ELIZABETH: Not serious.

FATHER: You don't think so? You think he's not serious.

ELIZABETH: He plays games and he tells jokes. When the time comes to say anything serious it's as if…

SON: Oh, for heaven's sake!

FATHER: No. No. Go on.

ELIZABETH: Well, it's as if there was something stopping him. All the time…

FATHER: Is that so? I wonder why that should be…

ELIZABETH: Well, I should think you'd know.

FATHER: Why?

ELIZABETH: Because you've never really said anything serious to him, have you? No one here ever says anything. They tell stories and they make jokes – and something's happening.

SON: Elizabeth. It doesn't always have to be said.

ELIZABETH: Sometimes. Sometimes it has to.

FATHER: Very well. What would you like to hear from me? What words – of wisdom?

Silence. They all look at the FATHER. He rises, moves up-stage and sings softly.

> 'She was as bee-eautiful
> As a butterfly
> And as proud as a queen…'

The SON rises and moves down.

The MOTHER and ELIZABETH exit.

SON: (*To the audience.*) He had no message. I think he had no belief. He was the advocate who can take the side that comes to him first and always find words to anger his opponent. He was the challenger who flung his glove down in the darkness and waited for an argument. And when the children came to see him he told them no more, and no less, than he'd told me…

A young GIRL and TWO BOYS enter.

FATHER: Ha, ha, and who have we here?

GIRL: I'm Daniel…

FATHER: Oh really, and you're…

FIRST BOY: (*Falsetto.*) And I'm Jennifer.

GIRL: I'm Daniel, honestly.

SECOND BOY: She's a liar.

FATHER: Oh, come now. I mean, if she says she's Daniel – shouldn't we take her word for it?

FIRST BOY: Tell us again…

FATHER: About what?

SECOND BOY: The Macbeths…

GIRL: (*With relish.*) Yes, the Macbeths!

FATHER: Dunsinane! What a dreadful place to stay…for the week-end. Draughts. No hot water. No wireless, and the alarm bell going off in the middle of the night when you least expect it. And finally…the dinner party!

GIRL: Go on! Tell us!

BOTH BOYS: Tell us…

FIRST BOY: About the dinner party!

FATHER: Oh, a most embarrassing affair. Dinner with
the Macbeths. And everyone's sitting down…quite
comfortably. And his wife says, 'Come and sit down, dear.'

FATHER / CHILDREN: (*Together.*) 'The soup's getting cold…'

FATHER: And he turns to his chair and sees – someone
– something horrible! Banquo! (*His voice sinks to a terrifying
whisper.*)

> 'The time has been
> That, when the brains were out the man would die
> And there an end, but now they rise again
> With twenty mortal murders on their crowns
> And push us from our stools…'

SON: I used to scream when he did that to me.

*The CHILDREN are quiet. The FATHER mouths stories to
them.*

(*To the audience.*) His mind was full of the books that he'd
read as a boy, lying in the hot fields in his prickly Norfolk
jacket. He told them of foggy afternoons in Baker Street
and sabres at dawn at Spandau Castle, and Umslopagas
and Alan Quartermaine and She Who Must Be Obeyed.
He spoke to them of the absurdities of his life…

FATHER: My old father was a great one for doing unwelcome
acts of kindness! Recall his rash conduct in the affair of my
Uncle George's dog…

*During this story which the CHILDREN know by heart, they
prompt him.*

SECOND BOY: It's the dog!

FIRST BOY: Go on about the dog.

FATHER: My poor Uncle George fell on evil days – and had
to sell his faithful pointer. And my father, thinking Uncle
George was heart-broken, went furtively about – to buy the
animal back. It was a most…

FATHER / GIRL: (*Together.*) Lugubrious hound...

FATHER: With a long powerful rudder! It seldom or never smiled. It was not so much dangerous as...

FIRST BOY: Depressing!

FATHER: Depressing indeed! And when he saw it again my Uncle George took himself off to Uxbridge where he got himself a post with good prospects and diggings at which, unfortunately, animals were not permitted. He shed no tears, to my old father's great surprise, at this second parting from his dumb friend who then took up residence with us. A most...

FATHER / CHILDREN: (*Together.*) Unwelcome guest...!

ELIZABETH enters with three waterproofs.

ELIZABETH: Come on, now. It's time to go home.

GIRL: Oh, no Mum. It's the one about the dog...

SECOND BOY: Let's finish the dog.

ELIZABETH: Oh, the dog!

FATHER: We offered the dog to anyone who would provide a good home for it. Then we said we'd be content with a thoroughly bad home for the dog. (*He laughs.*) Finally, we had to pay someone a large sum of money to have the animal taken away. But my mother and I used to remember terrible stories – about faithful hounds that were able to find their way home...

FATHER / CHILDREN: (*Together.*) *Over immense distances*!

ELIZABETH: Come on now, we must go really.

The MOTHER enters carrying a diary and joins the others in waving. The FATHER, ELIZABETH and the CHILDREN exit.

The MOTHER sits at the table. The SON moves down, facing the audience.

The lights change.

SON: The enormous garden became dark and overgrown in spreading patches. My father continued, daily, to chronicle its progress in the diary he dictated to my mother.

MOTHER: (*Reading from the diary.*) 'June twenty-fifth. We put sodium chlorate on the front path. We had a raspberry pie from our own raspberries. The dahlias are coming into flower. The jays are eating all the peas...'

SON: Willow herb and thistles and bright poppies grew up. The fruit cage collapsed like a shaken temple and wood supported the tumbled netting. The honeysuckle and yew hedges grew high as a jungle, tall and dark and uncontrolled, lit with unexpected flowers...

MOTHER: (*Reading.*) 'Thomas came and we saw him standing still among the camellias...'

SON: A boy was hired to engage the garden in single combat. His name was not Thomas.

MOTHER: (*Reading.*) 'July fifteenth. We planted a hundred white begonias and staked up the Malva Alcoa. A dragon-fly came into the sitting-room. Thomas was paid. Am laid up. The pest officer arrived to eliminate the wasp nests.

The SON goes out and returns with the FATHER in a wheelchair. ELIZABETH enters with a book.

Unhappily we couldn't watch the destruction...'

SON: In the summer, with the garden at its most turbulent, my father became quite suddenly very old and ill...

ELIZABETH: (*Reading.*) '"What are you going to take for breakfast, Mr Phelps?" said Holmes. "Curried fowl, eggs, or will you help yourself?" "Thank you, I can eat nothing," said Phelps. "Oh, come. Try the dish before you." "Thank you, I would really rather not." "Well, then," said Holmes, with a mischievous twinkle. "I suppose you have no objections to helping me?" Phelps raised the cover, and as he did so, uttered a scream, and sat there staring with his face as white as the plate upon which he looked. Across the centre of it was lying a little cylinder of blue-grey paper...'

FATHER: (*Breathing with difficulty; gasping.*) The Naval Treaty!

ELIZABETH: Yes. (*She closes the book.*)

FATHER: I'm afraid – you find that story a great bore.

ELIZABETH: Of course not. It was very exciting.

FATHER: Dear Elizabeth. I'm so relieved to find that you can lie as mercifully as anyone.

ELIZABETH goes.

(*Suddenly with a great effort he tries to get out of the chair.*) I want a bath! Take me to the bathroom. Cretins!

The SON holds him, and pulls him gently back into the wheelchair.

SON: Sit down. Don't be angry.

FATHER: I'm always angry – when I'm dying.

The FATHER's breathing becomes more irregular, then calms down as he falls asleep.

SON: It was a hot endless night, in a small house surrounded by a great garden in which all the plants were on the point of mutiny.

There is a long pause. The SON looks down on the FATHER, who is now sleeping.

The DOCTOR comes in, wearing a dinner-jacket and carrying his bag. He nods to the SON and leans over the FATHER and feels his pulse.

Dr Ellis...

DOCTOR: We've got a territorial dinner. In High Wycombe...

SON: How is he?

DOCTOR: (*To the FATHER.*) Wake up! Wake up! (*To the SON.*)
Don't let him sleep. That's the main thing. Come on,
wakey, wakey! That's better...

SON: But do you think...?

DOCTOR: The only thing to do is to keep his eyes open.
(*He leaves FATHER's hand hanging over the arm of the chair.*)
There's really nothing else. (*He pauses.*) I'll come back in
the morning.

The DOCTOR goes. The MOTHER follows.

*The SON turns back to the chair, he looks at the FATHER and
speaks urgently.*

SON: Wake up! Wake up! Please! Please! Wake up! (*He pulls a
chair next to the FATHER and sits by him. He arranges FATHER's
hand on his lap, and nods off himself.*)

*There is a silence. Slowly the light fades over part of the stage
where they are. The SON sits up suddenly, leans over, rises and
moves down.*

I'd been told of all the things you're meant to feel. Sudden
freedom, growing up, the end of dependence, the step into
sunlight when no one is taller than you and you're in no
one's shadow. I know what I felt. Lonely.

The SON turns and walks slowly away as –

the Curtain falls.

Printed in the USA
CPSIA information can be obtained
at www.ICGtesting.com
LVHW020957171024
794056LV00004B/1200

9 781840 026573